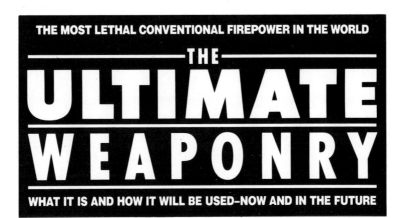

THE MOST LETHAL CONVENTIONAL FIREPOWER IN THE WORLD

THE ULTIMATE WEAPONRY

WHAT IT IS AND HOW IT WILL BE USED–NOW AND IN THE FUTURE

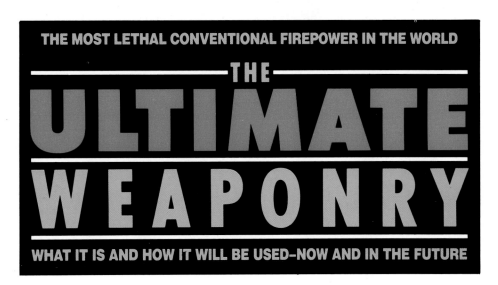

THE MOST LETHAL CONVENTIONAL FIREPOWER IN THE WORLD

THE ULTIMATE WEAPONRY

WHAT IT IS AND HOW IT WILL BE USED–NOW AND IN THE FUTURE

PADDY GRIFFITH

CONSULTANT DR JOHN PIMLOTT

ST. MARTIN'S PRESS

First published in Great Britain in 1991
by Sidgwick & Jackson Limited
Cavaye Place
London SW10 9PG

ISBN 0 312 06128 5

Printed by Eagle Colour Books Ltd,
Blantyre, Scotland.

Bound by the Bath Press, Bath, Avon

Editorial: Roger Ford, John Boteler, Chris Marshall, Rory Bridson
Picture Reasearch: Stasz Gnych
Design: Steve Wilson

Technical Illustrations: Graham Bingham
Battlefield overviews: Harry Clow

Picture Acknowledgments

Roger Ford 193 B/R. Robert Hunt Library 54 T/L, 121 T/R, 161
T. Hugh MacManners 26/27, 46 B/L, 49 B/R, 54 B/L, 61 B/R, 98
C/L, 130 B/R, 134 C/T, 137 T, 143 B, 148 B, 149 L, 158/9, 178/9,
189. 216 T, 217 B. Military Picture Library 111 B/R, 118, 124
B/L, 132 T/R. TRH Pictures 19 C/T, 20 T, 25 L, 31 T/R, 33 B/R,
34 B, 36 T/L, 37 C/B, 38 B/L, 40 B/R, 40 B/R, 42 B/L, 52 B, 55
T, 58/9, 59 T/L, 64 B/L, 65 B/R, 66 B, 71, 73 T/L, 76 T/L, 77 C/L,
82 C/B, 82 B/R, 89 B, 90 T/R, 92/93, 97 T, 100 T, 104, 115 T,
116 B/L, 119 B/L, 127 T, 128/9, 133 C, 141 B, 142 T, 152 T/R,
160 B/L, 162 B, 165 B, 166, 168 C/L, 168 B/R, 182 B/R, 187 T,
187 B/R, 188 B/L, 190, 197, 200, 201, 208/9,211, 214, 215 B, 215
C, 218, 219. TRH Pictures/DOD. 10 T/R, 11 T, 91 B/R, 108 B/R,
117 T/L, 126 B, 131 T/L, 144 C, 194 C/B. TRH Pictures/USAF 22
C/L, 24 T/R, 39 T/L, 46 B/R, 60 T, 64 T, 73 C/R, 86/87, 102 B/R,
103 B/R, 106/107, 116 R, 125 T, 192 T, 195 T. TRH Pictures/US
Army 40 T/L, 42 L, 44/45, 125 T, 140, 150, 155 T/L, 155 B, 172
B, 194. TRH Pictures/Y Debay 122 T, 145 C/R, 164 T, 178 T/L.

Cover: Multiple Launch System [Inset: Dragon ATGM]
Title Page: General Dynamics F–16 Fighting Falcon

CONTENTS

FOREWORD   6
(General Sir John Hackett)

INTRODUCTION   8

Chapter 1
ALL OVER BY CHRISTMAS   26

Chapter 2
COMMAND AND CONTROL   44

Chapter 3
THE AIR WAR   62
(Anthony Robinson)

Chapter 4
IS THE TANK DEAD?   84

Chapter 5
HELICOPTERS IN DANGER   104

Chapter 6
THE ARTILLERY BATTLE   126
(Hugh McManners)

Chapter 7
THE EMPTY BATTLEFIELD   148

Chapter 8
COMBAT ENGINEERING   170

Chapter 9
CASUALTIES AND REFUGEES   188

CONCLUSION   206

Bibliography   218
Glossary   220
Index   222

FOREWORD

by

General Sir John Hackett,

GCB; (KCB; CB); CBE; (MBE); DSO and BAR; MC; DL; FRSL

FEW would see in the title of this book any claim that in man's unceasing conflicts with other men, and the effort to bring into use more and more effective weapons of war, we have now reached finality, or even that it is in sight. Already we are at a stage where the wholly unrestrained use of the weapons now available could result in the virtual extinction of all human life upon this planet, but development of weapon systems and the research upon which it is based goes on. The search for greater effectiveness, accuracy, mobility, lethality and destructive power in offensive weapon systems persists in growing intensity. Even marginal improvements can be of high value and are eagerly sought after. In defence, whether of whole systems or parts of systems, or of objectives vital to an enemy, complete invulnerability lies like a will-o-the wisp beyond the horizon. We reduce vulnerability in any way we can. We do it, if possible, by evasion of attack, by protection against attack if it comes, by reactive response, preferably leaving the attacker worse off than before his attempt, by deception, by the use of obscurity and night vision, by the use of stealth techniques for the reduction, or complete elimination, if that were possible, of tell-tale invitations to attack. We use any means available, longing for the unattainable, the complete invisibility imagined only as in the gift of Wagner's *Tarnhelm*. We improve our communications, our information handling capability, our engineering and logistical technology and anything that can help towards the ultimate goal in battle - the unchallenged presence of an infantry soldier, armed only with a handheld weapon, upon a vital piece of real estate.

What this book offers, in the restless, endless search for the ultimate, is a valuable review of the present state of the art and a glimpse of some of the directions in which our search may now be moving. The contributors are not senior officers. The book does not emanate from the Royal Military College of Science at Shrivenham, where the technical training of officers in the Army, and a considerable part of the RAF, at University level, is now concentrated. This book has been put together by operators at the working level, men whose business is not so much to design and develop weapon systems as to make the very best use of what is put into their hands, while teaching others to do the same, and offering at the same time invaluable user comment on what they see developing.

It is a book which comes out of the Sandhurst stable, where the emphasis is less on the higher technology of war than on warlike practice in the field at lower working levels of command. It need hardly be stressed that in warfare it is at the lower levels of command that decision has to be sought. Without success in squadrons, batteries and companies, failure overall is quite inevitable. A survey of the state of the game as seen by highly experienced eyes at this level, deliberately avoiding authoritative input from above, must therefore be of great value, both to the battlefield practitioner and to the non-military observer who wants to know what, in this complex, costly and quickly changing scene, it is all about.

Men have been fighting other men from time immemorial, first with hand and foot and head in close physical contact and with such help as could be found in sticks and stones, and then with more effective tools. What Homer called the "pitiless bronze and grey iron" came into use. Flung spears and missiles from bow and sling were followed by armour and the use of animals. Gunpowder, steam, internal combustion, heavier-than-air flight, rations now canned and no longer on the hoof, electrics and electronics, automatic weapons - these are only some of the many inovations which have totally changed the whole aspect of warfare over only a very few centuries. Nuclear fissions and fusion brought in to war a radical change in kind, and with the development of chemical and biological weapons the ultimate in weaponry may be thought to have already been reached. Conflict will not cease however, and, although self-preservation may dictate avoidance of the ultimate, improvement in warlike techniques will continue to be sought. This book tells us, from the users point of view, where we have got to and where we seem to be going.

Very many topics offer themselves for enquiry and comment. Is the tank dead? What of air power and the land battle? Is the helicopter now the queen? Are we moving towards an empty battlefield, reshaped by the engineer, in which systems fight systems with minimal human involvement? What of artillery, and new systems replacing the antiquated practice of throwing at the chosen target containers packed with high exlosives? When do we see the railgun, and particle beam weaponry? The questions are legion and high among them is the future of command and control in a world increasingly dominated by automatic processes. One thing has to be remembered. Automatic data processing has reduced the area within which an intuitive human decision alone is valid. It cannot eliminate it. In the war of systems against systems, which increasingly becomes the pattern of warfare in our time, we must beware of the mortal danger lurking in the automatic response. Man must remain the final arbiter and at all costs resist becoming the powerless slave of his own ingenuity.

It is all the more important to survey current trends and progress in weapons technology because of the vast range of possibilities now opening up. These are far greater than can be exploited with the funds now available, or likely to become so, in any part of the world. This is, at least in part, the result of the feverish efforts of the Soviet Union to match the military strength of the USA and the huge impetus thus lent everywhere to military research and development. The historian is likely to see here a main cause of the disintegration of the USSR. Elsewhere an important result has been embarrassment in the determination of procurement priorities. They will tell you at the Royal Military College of Science of ten or twenty highly promising developments all now on the back burner for lack of funding. The Strategic Defence Initiative is very far from being the only sufferer here. The growing imperative of hard choices in procurement policy emphasizes the importance of well informed opinion at the level of the user about what is on offer, among growing numbers of options, all at soaring cost.

The appearance of this provocative book is most timely. It will lead the enquiring reader, military or civilian, to the asking of some awkward and important questions.

INTRODUCTION

In the two decades since 1970 there has been a quiet and largely unnoticed revolution in the technological resources that soldiers – from generals right down to the poor bloody infantry – have on hand for fighting their battles. This is a revolution that makes the Americans' vaunted high-technology helicopter army of the Vietnam years look distinctly obsolescent – and even perhaps entirely obsolete.

Below: Fist of steel in an iron glove. A British armoured brigade on exercise on the North German plain

Since the Americans withdrew from Vietnam, a huge number of 'emerging technology' (ET) weapons have been invented. Several have already been deployed, and almost all have been at least partially tested. The likely performance of each individual weapon is therefore reasonably well known. But we do not yet know exactly how all this sophisticated new equipment will hang together and interact in a real high-technology conflict. We do not know how they may be countered in real combat, or which of them will be the true war winners and which will turn out to be white elephants.

For example: will modern 'instant' air-scattered minefields be more or less effective against the latest main battle tanks (MBTs) and their mine counter-measures than were the laboriously hand-laid mines of 1941-5 against the very different tanks of half a century ago? Will battlefield lasers eventually turn out to be most important as direct fire weapons, as target designators, as secure communication links, or as blinding agents – and what precautions may practically be taken against them? Will the optimum combat aircraft of the future be manned or unmanned, sophisticated (but few) or 'cheap 'n' cheerful' (but plentiful) – and how easily will they defeat the air defence array they are likely to encounter? Will the anti-tank gun of the future rely on kinetic energy (KE), as in the past, or on plasma beams and other assorted possible new death rays?

But perhaps the major question is whether or not tactical radio communications will be possible at all in the face of massive professional jamming. If they ultimately turn out not to be, then almost the whole theoretical basis of modern tactics will be swept away at a stroke. The development of an entire generation of 'state-of-the-art' weaponry will suddenly be seen to have been a hideous blind alley – an anachronism far more gigantic and damaging, in its way, than was the widespread training of infantry to form squares against cavalry in the 1920s, not to mention the building of the Maginot Line.

As the world's armies enter the 1990s, they are facing a profound technical military conundrum. Truth to tell, they cannot properly visualise what a future high-technology conventional battlefield will look like, any more than the armies of July 1914 could imagine the battlefield over which they were to fight for the next four years. Whether or not they

Above: A sign of the times? The heads of the US and Soviet armed forces, Admiral Crowe (left) and Marshal of the Soviet Union Akhromeyev

CONVENTIONAL FORCES IN EUROPE

East-West negotiations for mutual and balanced force reductions (MBFR, or MFR for those who do not believe in the concept of 'balance') were held in Vienna between 1973 and 1989 without coming to any firm conclusion. In 1989, however, new talks began that turned out to be much more positive. Also held in Vienna, they concerned reductions in conventional forces in Europe (CFE).

In late 1988 President Gorbachev announced some unilateral cuts in Soviet forces, then, in the course of 1989, specific ceilings were agreed. Still, at the beginning of 1991, the Warsaw Pact had the capacity to put something like 30,000 tanks into what was West Germany within a month, out of a total of around 51,000 tanks stationed west of the Urals. Western diplomats hope that a CFE agreement will see the number of Warsaw Pact tanks reduced to 20,000 west of the Urals, with NATO retaining up to the same number in Western Europe. Since NATO has around 17,000 tanks, of which perhaps 10,000 would be available for Germany, this would lead to a position not far from parity.

The current proposals also provide for each side to have 28,000 armoured troop carriers, 500 air defence interceptor aircraft, 4700 combat aircraft and 3800 attack helicopters. The Eastern bloc refuses to count its numerous defensive fighters in the equation, and so would retain numerical superiority in the air. Quite apart from this negotiation, the advent of a unified Germany means that we may see a demilitarized buffer zone at the heart of Europe. This has been suggested by some CFE negotiators, although at the time of writing the military status and alignment of the re-united Germany remains unclear. Nevertheless, should the storm clouds return and Germany become a battle-ground, even under CFE there would still be very large forces available to fight a war there. After all, Hitler was able to defeat France in his 1940 *blitzkrieg* using a total of just 3000 tanks.

Above: The beginning of the end of the Cold War. Former US President Ronald Reagan (left) greets Soviet leader Mikhail Gorbachev in December, 1987. Almost three years later the Treaty of Paris formally ended 40 years of impasse

consciously know it, therefore, the world's more advanced armies may well be teetering on the brink of a technological abyss very similar to the one into which their counterparts fell on the outbreak of World War I. With the new technologies must come changes in training and tactics as the soldiers struggle to stay abreast of the most advanced military practice.

Modern war: more of the same, or something completely different?

But if weapons, tactics and training are in a state of flux, what of the basic plan, or 'doctrine', that an army embraces to fight its wars? It has generally been believed that the only way in which a war can ultimately be won is through mounting a successful offensive. No matter how effective one's defensive battle may be, it cannot on its own 'bring the war to the enemy', or completely destroy him, unless it is supplemented by some sort of attacking move. Therefore, efficiency in the assault has been seen

as the touchstone of military competence, and it has often been claimed that truly high military morale can be achieved only in the offensive, especially when the attacking army enjoys surprise and has wrested the initiative away from the enemy.

The problem, however, is that reckless assaults tend to result in more casualties than do careful tactical defensives, thereby rather quickly demoralising the attacker and giving correspondingly high reassurance to the defence. Thus it is not good enough just to recommend the offensive on every occasion – as the French came close to doing in 1914, and as, in recent times, both the Soviets and the Israelis have sometimes seemed wont to do. In the October War of 1973, the Israeli tactic of having tanks forge ahead and leaving the infantry behind led to problems in Port Suez, for example. When the Israeli armoured spearhead arrived there, what infantry there was with it dismounted too late from its carriers. In the maze of streets, Egyptian anti-tank teams took a heavy toll of both tanks and infantry as a result.

Between the end of World War II, in 1945, and 1988, the last year for which figures are available, there were no less than 93 wars in one degree or another, resulting in some 18,000,000 deaths and untold lesser casualties. Most of these will have been innocent civilians, caught up in a war not of their own choosing.

Today, there are a score of regions of the world where two or more groups are in conflict; in any or all of these the dispute could expand to include third parties and blow up into full-scale warfare.

1. The Caribbean Rim includes El Salvador, Nicaragua, Panama, in dispute with the United States; Cuba, whose Communist government has been a 30-year annoyance to the US, and Haiti, which has not been stable since the death of dictator "Papa Doc" Duvalier.

2. Northern South America includes Colombia and Peru, where both Communist insurgents and cocaine producers threaten the legitimate governments.

3. Southern South America includes Argentina, which has internal problems, and the Falkland Islands, over whose possession Argentina went to war with the United Kingdom.

4. North West Africa includes Morocco, Mauretania and Western Sahara, where border disputes have reached genocidal proportions.

5. North Africa includes Libya, seen for so long as the 'mad dog' of the Mediterranean, and Chad.

6. East Africa includes Ethiopia, Uganda, Somalia and Sudan, where civil wars have cost millions of lives in famine and pestilence.

7. The Baltic States of Estonia, Latvia and Lithuania are desperately trying to secede from the Soviet Union, against the latter's wishes.

8. Central Europe includes Poland, Czechoslovakia and Hungary, where political and economic problems are uppermost in people's minds, and Albania, Yugoslavia and Romania, where factionalism threatens national unity.

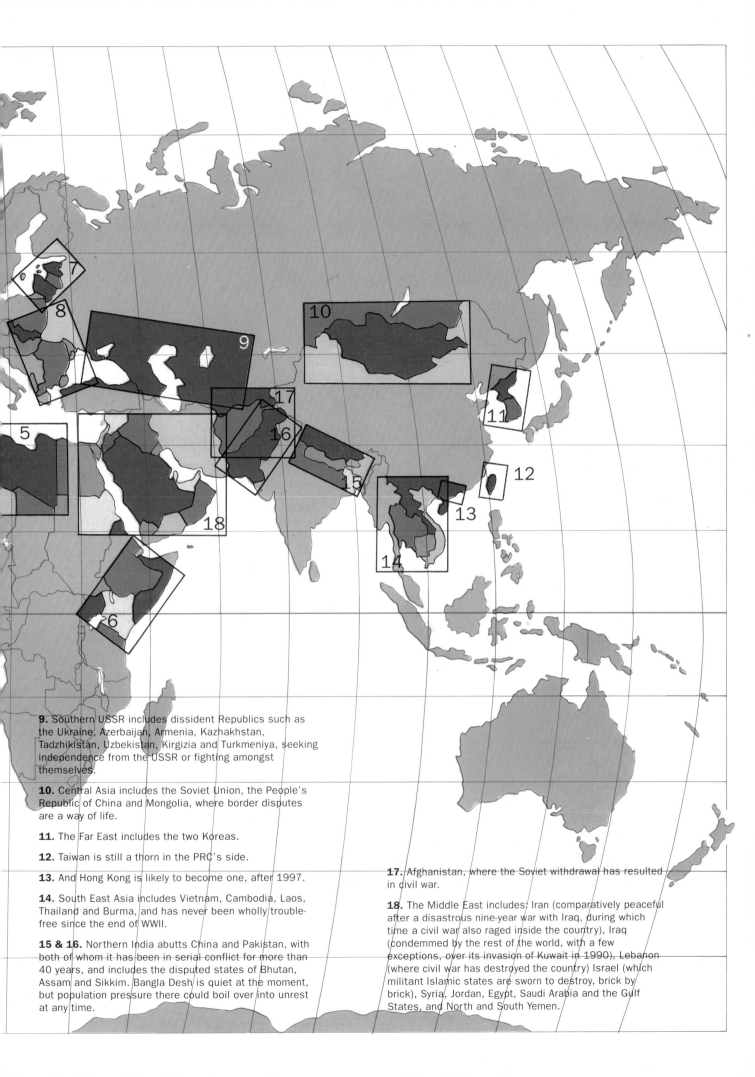

9. Southern USSR includes dissident Republics such as the Ukraine, Azerbaijan, Armenia, Kazhakhstan, Tadzhikistan, Uzbekistan, Kirgizia and Turkmeniya, seeking independence from the USSR or fighting amongst themselves.

10. Central Asia includes the Soviet Union, the People's Republic of China and Mongolia, where border disputes are a way of life.

11. The Far East includes the two Koreas.

12. Taiwan is still a thorn in the PRC's side.

13. And Hong Kong is likely to become one, after 1997.

14. South East Asia includes Vietnam, Cambodia, Laos, Thailand and Burma, and has never been wholly trouble-free since the end of WWII.

15 & 16. Northern India abutts China and Pakistan, with both of whom it has been in serial conflict for more than 40 years, and includes the disputed states of Bhutan, Assam and Sikkim. Bangla Desh is quiet at the moment, but population pressure there could boil over into unrest at any time.

17. Afghanistan, where the Soviet withdrawal has resulted in civil war.

18. The Middle East includes: Iran (comparatively peaceful after a disastrous nine-year war with Iraq, during which time a civil war also raged inside the country), Iraq (condemned by the rest of the world, with a few exceptions, over its invasion of Kuwait in 1990), Lebanon (where civil war has destroyed the country) Israel (which militant Islamic states are sworn to destroy, brick by brick), Syria, Jordan, Egypt, Saudi Arabia and the Gulf States, and North and South Yemen.

Although no strategic or operational surprise is possible under these circumstances, a commander may still attempt to achieve 'tactical surprise' – for example, by using multiple feints to confuse the enemy's intelligence picture, or by driving obviously towards one objective but then veering off sideways at the last minute to strike at another unsuspecting position. A classic Soviet technique is to assault over terrain that the enemy has assessed as impassable or almost so. In its whirlwind advance into Manchuria in August 1945 the Red Army completely surprised and outflanked the Japanese by pushing a major armoured spearhead through the Great Hingan mountains, using petroleum, oil and lubricants (POL) replenishment by air on the far side. The Japanese had expected none of this, imagining the mountains to be impassable to armour, rather as the French and Americans had imagined the Ardennes to be in 1940 and 1944 respectively.

In his memoirs of the great Soviet offensives into Poland and Germany in 1944-45, Marshal Chuikov assures his readership that a search for near-impassable terrain was standard practice in the planning of any offensive. There is much truth in the argument that 'the only bad terrain is terrain held by the enemy', and the Russians, more than anyone, have equipped their armoured forces to traverse the most unforgiving of hills, forests and rivers. These forces are lavishly provided with mine- and obstacle-clearing equipment, and have an impressive range of advanced bridges.

misleading signal traffic and the establishment of dummy units – complete with skeleton HQ staffs, dummy vehicles, new roads, pipelines and the like – combined with careful concealment and radio silence by the real spearheads that are preparing to strike from an unexpected direction. All of these techniques were widely used by both sides during World War II, and they have since been refined further– especially in the field of electronic warfare.

Yet an attack must also possess the flexibility to tackle prepared defences head on, on those occasions when something goes wrong with plans to avoid, encircle or pre-emptively smash through enemy strongpoints. For this type of operation the troops must be ready to mount a more formal and careful style of action – the 'set-piece assault'. This must be the 'worst-case scenario' for an attacker: a battle in which no strategic or operational surprise is achieved but where the defender must still be prised out of strongly fortified positions.

Deception techniques are a cheap way to buy time for an attack

In this type of operation the high command will have a much greater voice in tactical affairs than it does for encounter battles. In the former type of operation, the attackers' command staff must complete extensive and meticulous long-term preparation; must pre-brief and co-ordinate the spearheads and depth operations, so that they fully understand their own particular place in the overall picture but will hope to intervene relatively little on the day of the battle itself, leaving the tactical footwork to more junior commanders. For set-piece assaults, on the other hand, there must be meticulous planning of every detail – and especially generous logistic support – since this is potentially the most costly type of combat of all. Staff work must here reach down into the lowest levels of command, in order to maximise the chances of success, since brilliantly improvised manoeuvres will no longer be adequate on their own.

Above: Tanks of Rommel's 7th Panzer Division prepare to advance on the River Somme, in northern France, in June, 1940. A month earlier, the Germans had achieved complete operational surprise over the French by sending a solid phalanx of seven armoured divisions through the mountainous forests of the Ardennes – a region thought impenetrable to armour

Right: A German infantry commander from WWII signals his men to advance. One of the reasons for the Wehrmacht's success during that war was the high degree of initiative shown by even quite junior officers

At the end of the day, however, the formal set-piece assault will have to tackle enemy strong-points head on. This means that, as an opener, the strongest possible barrage of high explosive must be laid down from bombers, rockets and artillery. At the start of their Reichswald battle in early 1945 the British employed large numbers of all these, supplemented by almost everything else that could shoot, including Bofors anti-aircraft artillery (AAA) and Vickers medium machine guns. This was called a 'pepperpot' barrage, and it was entirely successful. The enemy troops in the front line were numbed and quickly surrendered. The only problem was that the bombardment had been so intense that fallen trees obstructed forward movement through the forest, while the town of Cleve was so badly cratered by bombing that it was impassable to the attackers' vehicles; a mighty traffic jam ensued, preventing the planned pursuit.

Today's artillery is capable of putting down even more terrible barrages. The Israelis working in the massive stone and concrete bunkers of their Bar Lev Line took a fearful pounding from the Egyptian guns during the shelling along the Suez Canal between 1970 and 1973. Although they were deeply dug in and not directly hit, the soldiers suffered badly from the shock waves and concussion of the shelling. In future wars it may be possible to kill defenders even in very deep bunkers by using fuel-air explosives (FAE) – clouds of explosive droplets that can penetrate concrete and masonry bunkers through ventilation systems and gun apertures before they ignite.

Developments in technology have not only enhanced the effectiveness of artillery fire, but also the distances at which it can be effective. The greatly increased range of modern artillery and rocket weapons means that the whole of even a very deep defensive layout can now be within the reach of an attacker's fire. Already in their 1972 Easter Offensive, the North Vietnamese were laying down intense barrages at ranges up to 27km, using the relatively lightweight Russian M46 130mm gun. Today the world's advanced armies regard such an outreach as routine, and can more than double it with specialised weapons.

The degree of surprise a force can achieve is conditioned by its reach

Achieving surprise is perhaps more important than ever on the modern battlefield, since the potential costs of a frontal slugging-match – which would take place were surprise not achieved – have risen in proportion to the rise in firepower and improvements in defensive capabilities. Mobile counter-moves can be very fast indeed, so an attacker must win the initiative especially quickly if he is to completely disarm them.

Yet as surprise has become more important, its achievement has become increasingly difficult. Major obstacles include the array of greatly enhanced surveillance technologies, which promise to give warning of impending threats well before they are launched. All advanced nations maintain

Right: The Battle of Kursk and (far right) the Israeli campaign to conquer Sinai. The Israelis were faced only with light opposition, and cut through it within four days. The Germans, on the other hand, were faced with a defensive force twice as strong as itself, where orthodox doctrine suggests at least a three-to-one superiority is necessary. They barely reached the third of the soviet forces' seven defensive belts

Right: German tanks would by-pass and seal off a strongpoint, leaving the infantry to deal with the besieged defenders. Few Wehrmacht infantry units were motorised, which meant that the infantry 'Landsers' walked – first across Poland, then across France, and later across Russia, almost as far as Moscow. Those that were left walked back

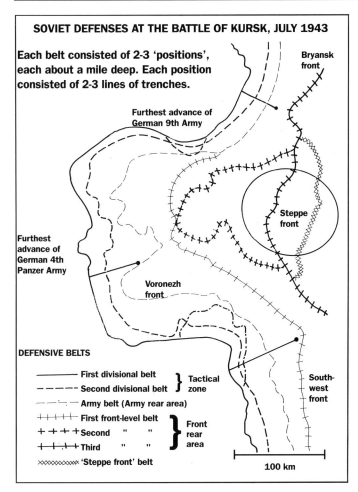

SOVIET DEFENSES AT THE BATTLE OF KURSK, JULY 1943

Each belt consisted of 2-3 'positions', each about a mile deep. Each position consisted of 2-3 lines of trenches.

Bryansk front

Furthest advance of German 9th Army

Steppe front

Furthest advance of German 4th Panzer Army

Voronezh front

South-west front

DEFENSIVE BELTS

— First divisional belt } Tactical zone
- - - Second divisional belt }
–·–·– Army belt (Army rear area)
+++++ First front-level belt } Front rear area
+ + + + Second " "
+·+·+ Third " "
×××××× 'Steppe front' belt

100 km

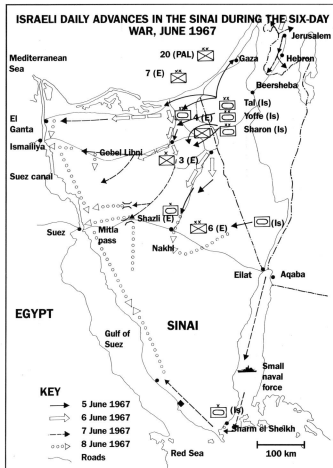

ISRAELI DAILY ADVANCES IN THE SINAI DURING THE SIX-DAY WAR, JUNE 1967

Jerusalem
Mediterranean Sea
20 (PAL)
7 (E)
Gaza
Hebron
Beersheba
Tal (Is)
4 (E)
Yoffe (Is)
Sharon (Is)
El Ganta
Ismailiya
Gebel Libni
3 (E)
Suez canal
Shazli (E)
6 (E)
(Is)
Suez
Mitla pass
Nakhl
Eilat
Aqaba
EGYPT
SINAI
Gulf of Suez
Small naval force
KEY
→ 5 June 1967
⇨ 6 June 1967
-→ 7 June 1967
ₒₒₒ▷ 8 June 1967
⌒ Roads
Red Sea
Sharm el Sheikh
100 km

vast electronic monitoring services (for example, GCHQ in Britain) that search the air waves for tell-tale signs of hostile plans or troop concentrations. Surveillance from satellites has made great strides forward in recent times, with increased speed, sophistication and reliability of reports, and improved mobility for receiving-stations. The days are gone when it took at least 24 hours to analyse the 'take' and then disseminate it to relevant tactical commanders.

Below the satellites, aircraft such as the American TR-1 tactical reconnaissance aircraft at high altitudes and drones lower down carry advanced multi-sensor imagers. TR-1s (the successors to the famous high-altitude U-2 'spy planes') form part of the precision location strike system (PLSS), under which they would fly in threes at high altitudes in pre-set 'race track' patterns. As soon as one aircraft latches on to a radar emission, which TR1s can monitor up to a distance of 320km, the other two will follow suit, thus providing a very precise 'fix' through triangulation. This result will be relayed instantly to the ground, theoretically allowing ET rockets to engage specific targets in less than 15 minutes. Equally the airborne warning and command system (AWACS) can monitor aircraft movements at very great ranges, although attempts to produce comparable airborne radars to identify ground movements at these distances have not been successful. At shorter ranges, however, the side-looking airborne radar (SLAR) and forward-looking infra-red (FLIR) is fully effective.

On the ground, there are many types of sensor that make the previously 'empty' battlefield appear very full indeed. Infra-red, passive thermal, acoustic, radar and other instruments – many of which may be unmanned and monitored at a distance – can shed light on the enemy's whereabouts and activities even in storms or on moonless nights. In Vietnam there was even a 'people sniffer' helicopter, equipped with sensors to detect human body odours...although apparently it had difficulty in distinguishing them from the smell of water buffalo!

Modern technology makes hide-and-seek a dangerous game

All this means that a surprise attack is harder to mount than ever before; and batteries of surveillance and monitoring equipment may be complemented by other conditions or devices which reduce the opportunities still further. For instance, where a defender has good surveillance methods and a wide 'no-man's-land' or 'buffer zone' that an attacker must cross before making contact, he can be reasonably confident that he will receive adequate warning. This is doubly true when there is a relatively stable political relationship between two possible antagonists. For example, a Chinese invasion of Russia would today be unlikely, and if launched, would probably fail to achieve surprise. The same is the case for an Egyptian invasion of Israel, though here there is an added safeguard. In very sensitive areas of the world, diplomatic

Above: Keeping front-line vehicles supplied with fuel will be one of the most difficult tasks facing a modern army

On the other hand, a country's surveillance cover might be incomplete; take, for example, the Ugandan air defences facing Israel's Entebbe raid of 1976, or the PLO in Lebanon facing Operation Peace for Galilee in 1982. Or the defending army may be deployed well forward in a linear formation that may be quickly penetrated by attacking spearheads. In this way Syria was able to reach Israel's Golan Heights defences quickly in 1973, and the Germans rapidly smashed through Russian lines along their border in 1941, while in the past 30 years NATO's potentially fragile 'forward defence' has always had to be covered by an exceptionally high level of surveillance. Then, there is the political scene to be considered. Stable political relations between countries lessen the likelihood of a surprise attack being successful, whereas volatile political conditions have the opposite effect. It is no coincidence that most surprise attacks in recent times have been in the Middle East. In future there may be a similarly volatile political scene in Eastern Europe and elsewhere.

Yet the fact remains that surprise can seldom be 100 per cent complete, and the best the attacker can realistically hope for is to allow the enemy to find out as little as possible about what his true objectives are – by reinforcing a false picture in the enemy's mind; by reducing the number of tell-tale signatures that are revealed to him, and by delaying the moment at which such signatures can be detected.

supervision may be set up to monitor a particular situation. Such machinery has existed to watch the Sinai desert since the Camp David agreement of September 1978 between Israel and Egypt, and a similar watchdog has, to a lesser extent, been keeping an eye on central Europe since the Helsinki accords of 1975 between NATO and the Warsaw Pact.

SOVIET DOCTRINE
The Continuity of Soviet Doctrine

Soviet doctrine for deep-striking, offensive armoured warfare was first outlined in the works of Triandafilov and Tukhachevskii during the 1930s, and was incorporated in the 1936 Field Regulations (known as PU36). Their ideas were shelved throughout Stalin's purges, the 1939 Winter War against Finland, and the initial German assault in 1941, but by the end of 1943 they had been rehabilitated in the light of battlefield experience. From then Soviet armoured offensives were designed to a set pattern that was practical, robust and highly successful.

Specific mathematical norms were established for each phase of battle. For example, Soviet practice in set-piece assaults was to select a sector for the breakthrough and there amass a ratio over the enemy of, on average, 5:1 in men, 8:1 in artillery, and 6:1 in tanks and assault guns. Each assaulting rifle division would be allocated a frontage of around two kilometres, and some 225 gun and mortar tubes (besides multiple rocket launchers) plus 19 tanks would be assigned to each kilometre of this breakthrough sector. On top of this an average of 64 tanks per kilometre were available to be committed

within 36 hours as mobile tank armies or other exploitation forces.

An instance of this system in practice was the Vistula-Oder operation of January and February 1945. On average 278 artillery tubes were lined up on each kilometre of front – which would have put them wheel-hub to wheel-hub had they been placed in a single line, rather than in the 'archipelago' layout that 20th-century artillery is able to use. There were also 22 tanks and self-propelled (SP) guns allocated to each kilometre in the initial tactical phase, with some 98 more per kilometre lined up in depth for the operational exploitation. This made a superiority over the enemy of 11.25:1 in artillery and 6:1 in tanks plus 7.25:1 in men; and the operation was supported by 4772 air sorties overall.

Using these norms the Soviet armour smashed through the German defences of the Vistula Line almost instantly, destroying its entire infantry garrison and most of the four Panzer divisions allocated for mobile defence. The front troops penetrated nearly 500km to the Oder Line – a breakthrough of record depth, in an area that had previously been thought

exceptionally well-defended. However, the Vistula-Oder operation actually failed to achieve its objective. Although the Soviet forces overran western Poland and eastern parts of the German Reich, it could still not punch through to Berlin itself. In 1945, therefore, even the Soviets' exceptionally high estimates of the basic forces needed to achieve breakthrough turned out to be somewhat less than a total recipe for victory.

Nevertheless, these doctrines have survived right up to the present day. In the 1950s they were adapted to cope with a nuclear battlefield, including a chequerboard of echelons in depth; then in the late 1970s they were converted back to provide a framework for purely conventional combat in the form of a 'single echelon' surprise assault.

Currently there is a new round of revisions under way that is intended to accommodate both ET weapons and the newly altered political map of Eastern Europe. Although Soviet doctrine is thus being taken in the direction of Kursk-style 'defensive defence', it will still retain a strong emphasis on fast armoured counter-attacks.

The problem is that there are so many different parts of the enemy's military and political machine to be taken unawares that at least some of these will almost inevitably find out at least a little of what is going on, and attempt to alert other departments.

Success in combat operations calls for more than just surprise and effective firepower. Warfare has always imposed great demands on wakefulness. Night has never stopped the artillery from firing, and darkness used to be an invitation to infantry to move because of the protection it provided. Indeed, the Israeli infantry, drawing partly on the British example in two world wars, particularly prided itself on its night-fighting skills, as the Israelis explained after their 1967 victory, and admirably illustrated in many a commando raid. Today the problem of sleep deprivation among troops is spreading to tank crews as high-tempo offensive moves, envisaged in both Soviet and US doctrines, call for a round-the-clock 'continuous battle' in which not only infantry and artillery but also armour participate.

The stamina of the men behind the equipment will be a ruling factor

In past wars armour often made night marches out of contact with the enemy in order to win positional advantage for a dawn attack; to that extent the continuous battle is no novelty for tank crews. However, in those days, when they were close to the enemy, being blind and vulnerable to infantry tank-killer teams armed with satchel charges, bazookas or RPGs, they would laager during the hours of darkness.

Admittedly, much of the night might well have been occupied in mechanical repairs and maintenance, but this was a very different level of activity from combat itself. The introduction of the infra-red sight (as used, for example, by the Syrians on the Golan Heights in the 1973 Arab-Israeli War) and more recently of the extremely efficient passive thermal imager changed all that by giving tank crews greatly enhanced night visibility.

It is ironic that the very technology – the passive thermal imager – that has made tanks able to fight at night has placed a large question mark over the place of the tank in modern war, by striking at its very mobility. At rest and waiting in ambush the thermal signature of a tank can be damped down by modern multi-sensor camouflage nets, such as the Diab-barracuda.

But these nets must be dismantled when the tank moves and the thermal image from its exhausts can once again be picked up. This means that tanks are more visible when mobile than when at rest, which in turn means that it is much more dangerous for

Right: Polish combat engineers assist in ferrying a T-72 tank across a river

Below: The higher the echelon, the further in front the commander must plan. Really fast-moving actions will tax both the intelligence-gathering and the decision-making processes

PLANNING AHEAD

The Corps commander, who is running the entire battlefield, can be expected to place his headquarters anything up to 100km behind the FEBA, for security reasons and to be sure of seeing the widest possible picture of events. He will have to plan for contingencies perhaps 36 or 48 hours ahead. The assets under his control range from air strikes, perhaps launched from a continent away, to *coup de main* attacks by Special Forces squads or infantry platoons. Tying all the information together into a cohesive whole is the most difficult job of all.

FEBA

Conventional artillery gives short or long-range support, but needs intensive logistic back-up

Strategic choke points, such as mountain passes or river crossings, can damage the logistics chain

Mech Infantry Bgd   Armoured Bgd   Divisional HQ

Corps Commander, perhaps 100km behind FEBA

Infantry units in FEBA

MLRS strikes deep into enemy rear, but eats up resources

Strategic attacks using missiles or aircraft may be launched from thousands of miles away

FEBA

THE PASSAGE OF LINES

To keep up the momentum of a battle, commanders have to replace exhausted troops with fresh ones without losing any of the impetus of their attack. This operation is called 'the passage of the lines', and its success or failure will obviously have a critical effect on the outcome of the battle as a whole.

During World War I, problems of command, control, communications and terrain made the passage of lines very difficult, and many attacks failed as a result. At Cambrai in 1917, for example, the British cavalry could not get through the initial wave of tanks and infantry to complete what should have been a victorious breakout. As a result the Germans were able to consolidate their resistance in the final line of their defences. The lesson was not lost on the British commanders. At Amiens the following year the cavalry was properly fed through the initial assault and did great damage to the German rear. Unfortunately there was not enough cavalry to turn the battle decisively in favour of the British forces.

In World War II, the passage of the lines was a key part of Soviet doctrine. Each unit was allocated enough ammunition and fuel to fight a particular type of battle for a set time. When that time was up, the unit was regarded as exhausted, and a fresh one was sent through to replace it. Great care went into the timing, planning and execution of these manoeuvres: police were deployed to prevent traffic jams, and the troops' proficiency in march discipline and flag signalling was crucial.

Today, successful passage of the lines is vital. The relative efficiency of the two sides in carrying out the manoeuvre will go a long way to deciding the outcome.

tanks to move than to halt – by day no less than at night – even though they can now fire accurately on the move, as they could never do before.

Although nocturnal fighting now seems to be technically as possible as day fighting for all three main arms, there is still the considerable question of whether the soldiers have the physical stamina to fight this sort of 24-hour battle. In the 1973 October War, for example, sheer fatigue often persuaded the two sides to agree – tacitly but mutually – to 'switch off' each night. On the other hand, against this, there is scientific evidence that most troops can in fact keep going for a few days with only an hour or two of sleep per day. Guderian's spearheads at the Meuse crossing in early May 1940 went for six nights without much sleep in the decisive battle of the French campaign, but had to slow down for a few days thereafter.

But even if troops and machines can theoretically keep going 24 hours a day, can sufficient supplies to maintain men, artillery and now tanks be transported around the battlefield? Wars end quickly if the initial thrust can be pushed through to a successful conclusion, but if an attack runs out of fuel at a key moment, it will be stopped just as effectively as if it had met unexpectedly strong enemy resistance – as the Germans discovered in their Ardennes offensive of Christmas 1944.

A US armoured division requires 17,300 gallons of fuel per hour

The logistics departments of the advanced armies are today run in a scientific fashion and backed by the same computerised and mechanised technology as any major warehousing and distribution system. Nevertheless in mobile operations immense strain is placed on the transport services, both by the sheer weight of supplies that must be carried and by the unpredictable moves called for in a fluid situation. With modern long-range firepower, moreover, unarmoured transport vehicles are desperately vulnerable, especially the large 40-ton 'juggernauts' that armies are increasingly using.

The fact is, however, that there is at present no substitute for these soft-skinned road vehicles. Ammunition can be transferred quickly to lorries on special pallets by the use of purpose-built lifting devices, and offloaded just as fast at gun positions, but trucks are still required to convey it to the gun line. Advances have been made, however, in the field of fuel transport, with advanced extendable pipelines for POL now in service that can bring

Below Left: A British Skynet 4 satellite in the course of testing. Three such satellites, in geo-synchronous orbit, provide secure and reliable strategic and tactical communications for the British armed services worldwide

The strategic HQ (A) receives information from Special Forces (1), via communications satellites (1A), from surveillance satellites (2), and from high-speed, high-altitude 'spyplanes' (3). The army group, or theatre, HQ (B), receives information from aircraft listening to enemy communications and radar emissions (4), and from 'AWACS' radar-surveillance aircraft (5). It can also task low-flying photo-recce aircraft (6), as can the corps HQ (C). This also receives information from dedicated jamming-detection (7) and stand-off radar aircraft (8), together with drogues and RPVs (Remotely Piloted Vehicles) (9), corps-level reconnaissance units – often including helicopters (10) – and the artillery's counter-battery radars. Signals units monitoring enemy radar traffic (12) report back to corps HQ, or divisional HQ (D). This will also receive information from its own recce units and maybe artillery RPVs, but its main source is from front-line units and observers (13), (14) and (15), using the assets shown in the accompanying box

Above: A Grumman E-2C Hawkeye Airborne Early Warning aircraft taxis towards the catapult prior to taking off from the *USS John F Kennedy*. The Hawkeye can detect aircraft 500km away. The Israelis used them to good effect in their battles with the Syrian Air Force over the Lebanon in 1982

to require between 1375 and 3100 tons of artillery ammunition alone; and in the Vistula-Oder operation of early 1945 the Russians expended no less than 315,000 projectiles in only the first 25 minutes of fire preparation. Unfortunately in almost every 20th-century war the logistic requirement has turned out to be much greater than predicted, especially for ammunition. In the October War of 1973, both sides had planned for at least three weeks' fighting, but were already running low after just 10 days, while for much of the 1980-88 Gulf War, Iran and Iraq were making do with very inadequate scales of ammunition, in scenes reminiscent of the general European shell shortage of 1915.

Thus the successful prosecution of a battle requires not only that supplies be efficiently moved about the battlefield, but also that adequate supplies be set aside in the first place. However, a barrier to the latter is that the manufacture and resupply of advanced modern munitions is enormously expensive, which gives rise to the temptation to stockpile unrealistically small quantities. Once again the 1973 War may be cited as an example: in that conflict there was an especially acute shortage of advanced anti-tank and surface-to-air missiles.

Defence in depth is more effective than packing a front

So far the emphasis has been on the problems faced by an attacking commander; the defending general has his problems too, and his plans to make. When faced with the possibility of massive deliberate bombardment, for example, a defending general must choose carefully how he will deploy his forces. In such a situation he seems to have several options open to him. On the one hand, he may rely on digging in his troops as deeply as possible, in something like the Bar Lev Line – although as outlined above, increased artillery firepower makes this a far from ideal solution. An alternative is to arrange defences in great depth, as the Russians did at Kursk – the 1943 battle that has undoubtedly made most impact on recent Soviet doctrine. However, the increased range of artillery has also called this option into question.

In the summer of 1943, the Germans wanted to pinch out the Kursk salient by mounting a twin offensive through its two shoulders, from Orel and Belgorod respectively. However, the operation was delayed for some three months while Hitler insisted on bringing up additional forces and the new Panther and Tiger tanks. By the time the attack actually started on 5 July, the Russians had long known of its details and had carefully prepared their defences, with strongpoints and minefields arranged up to 120km in depth. These were so arranged that the attacker's short-range artillery could tackle only a small part at any one time. Once he had dealt with each section of defence and made a 'bound' forward, the enemy would have to redeploy his guns to engage the next section. Although this entails the sacrifice of the front line by the defenders, the constant halts that the enemy is compelled to make fixes him and renders him ripe for a counter-attack, in this case in crushing style by massed armour.

truly prodigious volumes up to divisional rear areas. And this is just as well, for an American armoured division would need some 173,000 gallons of fuel for every 10 hours of tactical advance, with each of its M1 Abrams MBTs consuming a full load of 508 gallons within that time, while Soviet norms for an operation by a Front allow for the consumption of some 25,000 tonnes per day.

This assumes of course that the enormous quantities of supplies required by a fighting army are available. For example, a single deep attack by a modern US armoured division has been calculated

THE SURVEILLANCE ARRAY IN MODERN WAR

A
1A
2
3
4
5
6
B
7
8
9
1
XXX HQ
D
10
C
xx HQ
13
14
12
15
11

Seismic sensors
Radar
Thermal imager
Image intensifier
Binoculars/optical weapons sights

When it began, the German assault force contained over 1000 tanks, but it made heavy weather of the enemy infantry positions. It advanced less than 30Km during the first week – scarcely a *blitzkrieg* rate of advance – and was then halted in a massive armoured battle, principally around the village of Prokhorovka, as the Russians committed their reserve of over 3000 tanks. Three weeks after the battle had started the Germans were in full retreat towards the west, while the Red Army finally realised that it possessed both the numbers and the operational skills needed to defeat the Nazi invader.

The events of 1943 on the Eastern Front illustrate a third style of mobile defence. For between the surrounding of the German Sixth Army at Stalingrad at the end of 1942 right up to and beyond Kursk, the Germans fought a series of desperate thrust and parry defensive combats all along the front, giving an idea of what 'mobile defence' with armoured forces should be about. These actions, put into effect by the German generals Erich von Manstein and Hermann von Balck, have been carefully studied by both NATO and Warsaw Pact armies ever since.

In November 1942 the Soviet army perfected the successful operational doctrine that they have followed in general ever since. At Stalingrad, it used *maskirovka* to conceal the build-up of huge outflanking forces which smashed through the weak allied armies on either side of the German Sixth Army, thus putting it in a 'cauldron' from which there was no escape. Manstein took command of the relief attempts but at the same time, the Russians threatened a second and greater encirclement of the German Army Group A in the Caucasus.

It was during the successful fighting to extricate this army group that General von Balck's 11th Panzer Division used Manstein's technique of 'mobile defence', performing a sequence of illuminating defensive 'fire brigade' actions on the River Chir, in which the formation marched under cover of darkness each night to strike a Soviet spearhead at dawn. Often Balck would pin the enemy down with infantry, artillery and anti-tank guns in front, then manoeuvre armour to the rear. The Soviet forces would be shot up from behind, by what they had imagined was their own rear echelon. Without support, however, von Balck could not reverse the tide and the German forces at Stalingrad could not be relieved; they surrendered on 2 February 1943.

Above: Tactical mobility at the lowest level. An Australian trooper crawling under barbed wire during basic training. Stamina and fieldcraft skills often go hand in hand

Below: Soldiers also need stamina of a different kind. An American M60A3 crewman awaiting an order to move out

Manstein's use of a very mobile and hard-hitting 'fire brigade' defence was to be repeated many times during 1943 – sometimes at the level of battlegroups and divisions, sometimes at the level of Panzer corps or above. The technique should be set alongside several other German expedients that were also being used around this time, as Soviet assaults built up to a crescendo after their victory at Kursk. Around Orsha, for example, the German Fourth Army used a system in which enemy offensives were carefully predicted by intelligence, then troops were rushed across from quiet sectors to reinforce the threatened point, exploiting reserve positions dug to a depth of some 50km behind the front line. In the 1970s the US Army was to adopt a very similar doctrine under the name of 'active defense'.

Creative defense is often as mobile as attack

A daring World War II variant of active defense was demonstrated in Russia, East Prussia and finally outside Berlin by the German general Gotthard Heinrici. His technique, based on a German World War I model, was to work out as far as possible from intelligence reports when the Russian assault would start and then, a few hours before it began, evacuate his front-line positions apart from a few sentries and machine-gun crews. The main enemy artillery barrage, often the best and most carefully prepared blow in an assault, would thus fall harmlessly on the evacuated positions and the infantry attack that followed would be left denuded of artillery support when it finally came up against the real German position a few kilometres to the rear. Heinrici was using 'tactical agility' rather than

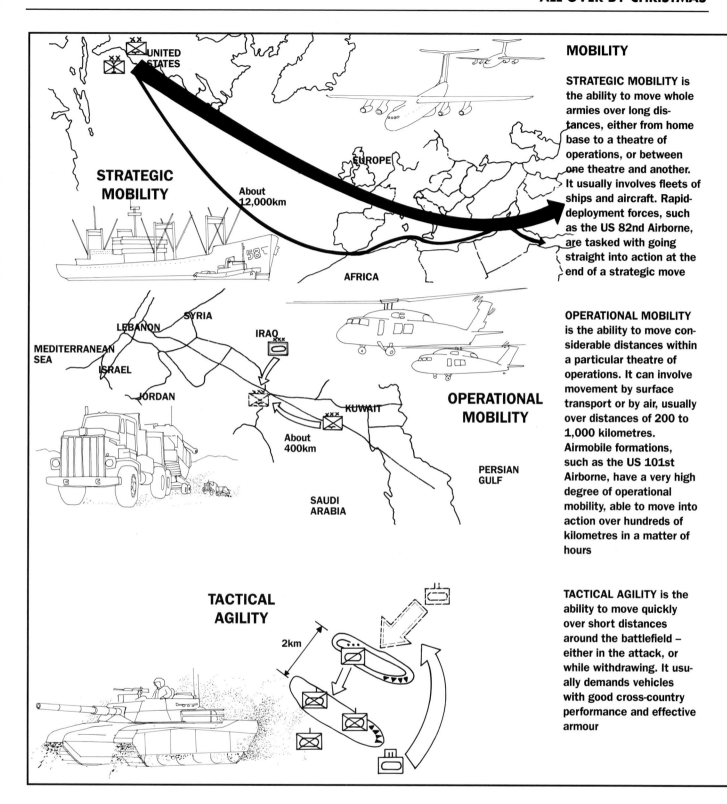

MOBILITY

STRATEGIC MOBILITY is the ability to move whole armies over long distances, either from home base to a theatre of operations, or between one theatre and another. It usually involves fleets of ships and aircraft. Rapid-deployment forces, such as the US 82nd Airborne, are tasked with going straight into action at the end of a strategic move

OPERATIONAL MOBILITY is the ability to move considerable distances within a particular theatre of operations. It can involve movement by surface transport or by air, usually over distances of 200 to 1,000 kilometres. Airmobile formations, such as the US 101st Airborne, have a very high degree of operational mobility, able to move into action over hundreds of kilometres in a matter of hours

TACTICAL AGILITY is the ability to move quickly over short distances around the battlefield – either in the attack, or while withdrawing. It usually demands vehicles with good cross-country performance and effective armour

STRATEGIC MOBILITY

About 12,000km

OPERATIONAL MOBILITY

About 400km

TACTICAL AGILITY

2km

UNITED STATES

EUROPE

AFRICA

SYRIA

LEBANON

MEDITERRANEAN SEA

ISRAEL

JORDAN

IRAQ

KUWAIT

PERSIAN GULF

SAUDI ARABIA

SUPPLY
The Concepts for Supplying Armies

Most armies organise their logistics 'from the bottom up' – front line units hold the transport resources and send back to rear depots when they need supplies. In Soviet-model armies, however, it is the HQs in the rear that hold the transport, and release it only to units judged to be of particular importance to the tactical plan.

This system allows senior commanders to concentrate resources at key points, and reinforce success in a fluid situation. It is less wasteful in supplies than systems where everyone has an equal right to top up – but it effectively denudes and abandons the units that are not considered worth replenishing.

the 'operational mobility' that Manstein and Balck had been able to employ. It may be that in future 'tactical agility' will be the only defence against a crushing deliberate attack.

In any event, on the modern battlefield, a large military formation, such as an army group, which is awaiting attack will have certain priorities built into its national or alliance-wide doctrines and plans. Such a formation would have its territory arranged in zones, each of which will be designated for a particular task or phase of the battle, and accorded a certain priority.

First, the most advanced zone is the 'deep surveillance zone', which extends into the enemy's territory and is intended to give early warning, thereby eliminating surprise. Once the battle has started, at least the forward parts of this zone will remain under surveillance to identify oncoming reinforcement echelons and developing thrusts.

Second, the enemy's territory will also be used for the 'interdiction battle' – that is, attempts to destroy or delay the second attack wave and support units coming forward behind the enemy's advancing front. The idea is to isolate the battlefield from outside help, in the same way that Montgomery's desert air force cut off Rommel's army from its fuel supply during the second battle of Alamein in late 1942. Today this could be achieved by modern ET weapons, which could launch devastating anti-armour strikes from as much as 300km behind the defenders' front line.

Third, along this front line itself there will be a zone for 'covering forces' – mobile armoured forces deployed to challenge and delay the initial enemy spearheads. Besides winning time for the main defences further to the rear, their job is to identify the precise size, direction and intentions of these enemy spearheads. In some cases this initial zone

Right: The Space Shuttle *Discovery* lifts off from Cape Canaveral. Though expensive, the Shuttle allows satellites to be put into precise orbit at short notice, like that placed to observe and report on the Persian Gulf in November 1990, following Iraq's invasion of Kuwait

Below Left: Aircraft such as the U-2 and the now-withdrawn SR-71 can obtain pictures like this within hours of the need arising. Flying at altitudes of up to 100,000 feet, they are invulnerable to normal air defences

may be fortified with strongpoints, anti-tank obstacles, and such like, although in the case of a surprise attack the problem will be how to man these positions quickly enough – and with sufficient troops. The USA has tried to solve this through 'graduated mobilisation response' (GMR). This is a phased mobilisation concept that allows partial local mobilisations to take place ahead of the general national decision to mobilise, thereby enhancing tactical readiness in the front line even before a suspected crisis has reached the President's desk.

Interleaved defense in depth requires careful planning

Fourth, behind the covering forces will be a 'main line of resistance' which – once again, if there is time to man it – should be held in force by major formations, including infantry and some of the less mobile armour, covered by extensive engineer work, such as minefields and demolitions. The task of these troops is to crush each oncoming spearhead in a set-piece battle. If the attacker has achieved a high level of surprise, however, this line may be full of holes, and a formless 'intermingled' battle will ensue, in which the attacker enjoys many advantages.

Fifth, integrated with, or held behind, the main line of resistance will be counterattack formations – reserves that will aid the defence at identified weak points, and destroy the attacker's shattered remnants where he has been halted. These forces may operate at a local level or at higher levels, all the way up to multi-corps counter-moves reaching far into the enemy's territory; they should be especially mobile and able to support themselves during a long move.

Sixth, and behind everything else, is the 'logistic rear' – the zone from which supplies and reinforcements are drawn to feed the fighting line. This zone will be pounded by the enemy's interdiction attacks and so must be defended: in modern war it will be more of an active fighting zone than was normal in the past. And its importance cannot be overstated: a well-sited defence that runs out of food before it runs out of men and weapons will be unable to sustain fighting morale. The Argentines found this out in the Falklands campaign of 1982, in which the efficiency of their food distribution to the defending troops left much to be desired.

The important questions for defensive war planning are: just how much of the available resources will be allocated to each of these zones? and how deep will each of them be? For example, in NATO there are certain assumptions that arise from the operational concepts accepted within the alliance. Thus, the concept of Forward Defence means that NATO would have wanted to fight the battle to defend West Germany in a strip of territory running along the border with the East – not deep inside West Germany. This might have helped to preserve German cities, but it brings some military disadvantages, such as a lack of room for manoeuvre, acceptance of war on German soil and a commitment to linear defence in an age of depth warfare.

It also places a relatively high priority on surveillance, and there will be a longer logistic chain to defend. But this may well be at the expense of the main line of resistance and – especially – of the counter-attacking reserves. Furthermore, the area of defence would be very narrow (50km deep at the most), and the forces to man it would have to move a long way to get into position; something that could prove fatal if an opponent did in fact achieve surprise. The American air-land battle (ALB) doctrine of the 1980s and the follow-on forces attack (FOFA) planning guideline for the 1990s both take forward defence even further, stressing the need to strike deep against Warsaw Pact second echelons, delaying and destroying them before they reach the main battle. Once again the main line of resistance might have to make sacrifices, but the hope is that by destroying the second wave, the US troops in the front line would not have too many enemy units to tackle at once and could fight to win against an isolated first-echelon force.

Modern reconnaissance techniques make surprise difficult to achieve

A future war will be finished off quickly only if the attacker can achieve a high degree of initial surprise, and follow that with extremely efficient logistics to keep his forces supplied with all they need through the full depth of the enemy's position. Careful *maskirovka* will have to go into the initial planning, after which junior commanders must operate loyally according to doctrine. Troops will have to make great efforts to maintain the momentum of the 'continuous battle', and they will need far greater provisions of fuel and ammunition than has been customary in the past.

DOES VICTORY DEPEND ON SURPRISE ?

The argument that a future war can be won only if the attacker achieves a very high degree of surprise is based on these suppositions:

• Emerging technology has helped make defensive warfare so effective that an attacker will commit his forces only if he is sure that he will catch his enemy off his guard, unable to bring his own arms to bear in time to defeat the assault

• Fashionable, peacetime military and political theories may cause a country to get its defensive priorities wrong – in which case he runs out of supplies, reserves or operational depth before he can blunt a surprise attack

• Sophisticated deception measures and *maskirovka* make surprise easier,

and launching an attack correspondingly more effective

• Surprise is an especially important ingredient of an attack against inexperienced armies who are unfamiliar with a real battlefield. The first battle of a war may then be its last

• New long-range emerging-technology weapons are ideal for making a mass pre-emptive strike against the full depth of the enemy's positions, crippling him almost before he is aware that he is at war

Arguing against the crucial importance of surprise are these arguments:

• Improved techniques of defensive warfare may make it harder to exploit surprise even if it can be attained

• A defending army with the correct doctrine will be able to sustain, supply and prolong the battle for a long time after the initial surprise has worn off

• All-weather, long-range battlefield surveillance technology is now so sophisticated that surprise is virtually impossible to achieve in the first place

• Potential defenders now understand the importance of surprise to an attacker so well that they are now taking comprehensive diplomatic, doctrinal, organisational and tactical measures to make it all but impossible

• Surprise can never be 100 per cent complete, and modern mobile armies can very quickly switch units from 'unsurprised' sectors to surprised ones

The nerve centre of a modern warship is the CIC, the Combat Information Centre. Above: The French carrier *Clemenceau's* CIC, showing integrated radar and automatic data-processing consoles. Even more than land- or air-based systems, ships depend on electronic sensors for their raw data

a headquarters. A commander cannot make meaningful decisions without knowing his superiors' intentions and the location and status of his own troops, together with their supporting arms and logistics, not to mention intelligence of the enemy, the weather and the terrain. His staff works assiduously to learn as much as possible of all these factors from the massive flow of information between the HQ and the subordinate units. But communications, vital as they are, cannot do the commander's job for him. The protean nature of battle dictates that he has no chance of ever learning all he needs to know – no matter how efficient the signals and intelligence network. At some point, he will be forced to cut short his deliberations and make decisions long before the picture is complete, and the

gaps in his knowledge – the 'fog of war' must be made good by plain old-fashioned intuition and guesswork.

Information lights a path through the fog of war

Once the commander has understood as much of the general picture as he can, he must decide what he can do to change it in his favour. For instance: intelligence has confirmed that an enemy motor-rifle regiment is rapidly approaching a division's forward defended localities down a narrow valley. The divisional commander may opt to wait and see what develops, thereby giving himself extra time for intelligence gathering and decision-making.

Above: Huge, terrestrial radar installations like this can 'see' even small objects to the limit of the earth's atmosphere. The familiar sweeping antennae have largely been replaced by fixed, phased-array antennae, in which a computer controls the 'movement' of the sensing processors from one vertical array element to the next, rather than shifting the whole antenna to create the same effect

Alternatively he may act pre-emptively to reinforce the threatened localities directly, to counter-attack, or to manoeuvre for a counter-stroke. Whichever course of action he chooses, he must give his own forces adequate warning, so that they are informed of the situation and the plan and not just overtaken by events. That in itself is a tall order, requiring still more communications traffic within a short timescale. And if additional units are to be committed to the battle, they must be given time to organise themselves into appropriate tactical groupings, top up with POL and ammunition in a leaguer area, and for their line of march to be reconnoitred and protected against both enemy surveillance and attack on the ground or from the air.

The higher the command level, the better the juggling act

This in itself is a massive task for an HQ staff that may be under attack, and it is only the beginning. If anything goes seriously wrong at any point along the way – for example, if a vital bridge is destroyed – a whole new command/decision cycle will have to initiated.

To cope with the demands of the modern battle, the commander must be both cool headed and far thinking. He must simultaneously remember what his subordinate units are doing and be able to give each one of them sound, clear orders at short

notice. If there is some unforeseen development in one sector, he must instantly analyse what it may mean for other sectors and pass on appropriate orders in good time. A commander may wish to improve his chances of controlling the battle by going forward to see for himself – in a jeep, a tank or a helicopter. There is a strong case to be made for this type of personal reconnaissance, if only because it gives the commander the opportunity to talk personally to the men on the ground, though doing so will cut him off from his HQ and staff, and effectively prevent him from exercising all his command functions.

It is perhaps an agressive commander's natural instinct, in any event, and there is plenty of historical precedent. Guderian led the *blitzkrieg* through France from the front; Rommel did the same in North Africa, and even Montgomery, the most conservative of men when it came to committing troops to battle, placed himself firmly in the forefront of the action. Often, the presence of the Commander in Chief boosts the men's morale considerably, even though it may actually degrade his own command ability – Wellington's performance at Waterloo springs to mind – and there will be times when engendering the will to fight and win is more important than retaining control of the battle. Colonel 'H' Jones, VC, realised this at Goose Green during the Falklands War, and pressed on with a personal attack that cost him his life.

IS COMMAND AND CONTROL STILL POSSIBLE ?

Modern weaponry and electronic counter-measures pose such a threat to modern armies' intelligence and communications that battle-field command and control may simply break down. Backing up this argument are these salient points:

• Tactical radio, especially VHF, may well be blown off the air from very early in the battle, leaving only cumbersome line-of-sight com-munications or satellite links – which them-selves may be shot down

• HQs are much more vulnerable than in past wars. They will be targeted by smart weapons launched at very long ranges

• The modern battle will be faster and more complex than ever before. It will demand an exponential improvement in analysing data and automatic data processing may backfire on itself, as increasingly complex systems are inevitably more prone to failure, while com-manders as well as computers may suffer from information overload

• Few of today's high-ranking officers have fought a real war. The habits of peacetime generalship are well-known enemies of wartime generalship

• Leadership 'from the front' is particularly dangerous, and puts the leader out of touch with the rest of the battle besides

But command and control may be easier and more effective than ever, for these reasons:

• New areas of the of the electromagnetic spectrum will be exploited for tactical commu-nications, and new ways will be found to make them easier to use

• Remote antennae, better protective tech-niques and more mobile command vehicles may allow HQs to stay one jump ahead of the enemy's weapons

• Improved data processing leads to a better analysis of complex information, and com-manders get an instantaneous ('real time') pic-ture of the battle as it develops

• Modern methods of personnel selection and vetting give us a better chance than ever before to appoint leaders who will perform well under stress of war

• Leading from the front is probably the best way to lead, especially within the doctrine of *auftragstatik* or 'mission analysis'

Right: Forward Observation Officers (FOOs) practising their skills on the range. The laser rangefinder/designa-tor, seen on the right, has revolutionised the FOO's working methods and has given him the capacity to make far more accurate judgments than were pos-sible in the past. One of the keys to success on future battlefields will be the speed and efficiency with which the information supplied by the FOOs can be acted upon by senior commanders. Given the weight of artillery fire available, especially from systems such as MLRS, then a well-timed artillery strike, say on a mecha-nised infantry brigade on the move, could very well destroy an entire formation within a matter of minutes

THE AIR WAR

Aircraft play a part in the land battle primarily through directly attacking enemy forces. They may operate in immediate support of friendly ground forces (close air support, or CAS), or in the rear areas of the battlefield (battlefield air interdiction, or BAI), or deeper within enemy territory (interdiction). In the last instance, strategic bombers may supplement the efforts of tactical attack aircraft, as happened in Vietnam and throughout the Southeast Asia conflict, and as is envisaged by the current United States Air Force doctrine and plans.

Below: The ominous shapes of two F-117A Stealth Fighters of the USAF. This was the first aircraft in the world whose chief design consideration was to reduce radar detectability – hence the unusual shape. The F-117A first saw action in Panama in 1989

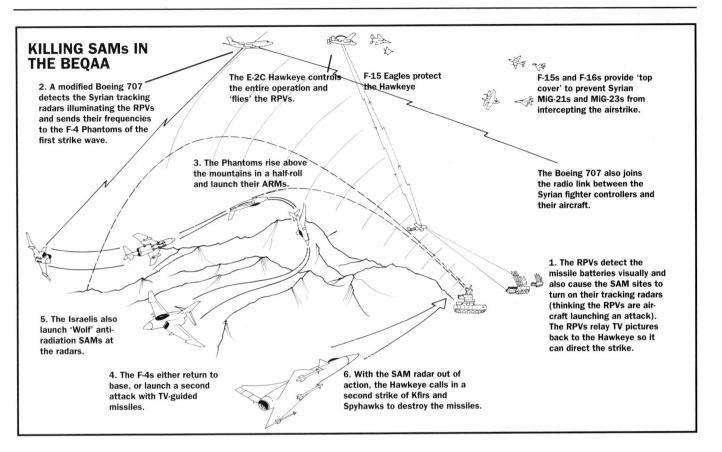

KILLING SAMs IN THE BEQAA

2. A modified Boeing 707 detects the Syrian tracking radars illuminating the RPVs and sends their frequencies to the F-4 Phantoms of the first strike wave.

The E-2C Hawkeye controls the entire operation and 'flies' the RPVs.

F-15 Eagles protect the Hawkeye

F-15s and F-16s provide 'top cover' to prevent Syrian MiG-21s and MiG-23s from intercepting the airstrike.

3. The Phantoms rise above the mountains in a half-roll and launch their ARMs.

The Boeing 707 also joins the radio link between the Syrian fighter controllers and their aircraft.

1. The RPVs detect the missile batteries visually and also cause the SAM sites to turn on their tracking radars (thinking the RPVs are aircraft launching an attack). The RPVs relay TV pictures back to the Hawkeye so it can direct the strike.

5. The Israelis also launch 'Wolf' anti-radiation SAMs at the radars.

4. The F-4s either return to base, or launch a second attack with TV-guided missiles.

6. With the SAM radar out of action, the Hawkeye calls in a second strike of Kfirs and Spyhawks to destroy the missiles.

Although both attack aircraft and escort fighters must carry EW equipment that can jam SAM and AAA radars, this individually-fitted equipment will not protect an attacking formation from these threats. So dedicated defence-suppression aircraft will join the escort force. The USAF designates such aircraft 'Wild Weasels'. Currently the USAF assigns F-4G Phantoms and F-16C Fighting Falcons to its Wild Weasel units, the two types operating together as 'hunter-killer' pairs. The Services Follow-on Wild Weasel project, set up to field a successor to the F-4G, has fallen foul of recent budget cuts, and so the present force is likely to continue in service until the early years of the next century.

The Wild Weasels operate at low level and on the flanks

The F-4G carries a complex threat detection system (the AN/APR-38), which is capable of locating and identifying a wide range of radars associated with ground-based SAM and AAA systems. Not only will the system give the range and bearing of these threats, but it will also indicate which of them is the most dangerous. The F-4G's backseater or 'Bear' can then deal with the trouble, either using his own stand-off or freefall armament, or by directing the accompanying F-16C against the enemy.

The F-16Cs are virtually standard aircraft, with only some changes in computer software required to suit them to the new role. They carry both freefall ordnance and anti-radiation missiles, with which to attack SAM and AAA sites and their associated radars, and (unlike the F-4G) also have a built-in gun armament. The Wild Weasels operate at low level ahead and on the flanks of the strike

force. They play a very dangerous game of cat and mouse with the ground defences, their primary objective being to create a safe corridor through enemy airspace for the strike force.

Specialised EW aircraft can also have a vital role in neutralising the enemy air defence forces, either through jamming their radars or by means of 'spoofing' tactics. For example, barrage jamming can be used to create a barrier behind which a strike force can assemble for its attack. Jamming escort aircraft, however, need to be able to perform better than most standard EW aircraft. The answer has been to use converted strike aircraft like the USAF's EF-111A Raven and the US Navy's EA-6B Prowler. The Raven's operations depend to a high degree on automation, since it carries only a pilot and one electronic warfare specialist. The Prowler is a more effective aircraft in this respect, since it can carry three specialist crew members, but it lacks the overall performance of its USAF counterpart.

Specialised diversions give the strike force valuable supprt

Other specialist aircraft can give the strike force valuable support. In-flight refuelling tanker aircraft, for instance, are often needed to provide the necessary range for a strike mission. During USAF operations over Southeast Asia during the Vietnam War they were particularly useful during the withdrawal phase of a strike, providing fuel to aircraft that otherwise would not have regained their bases. Then there are AEW aircraft, which monitor the progress of a strike at long range and if necessary provide advance warning of a developing threat from enemy interceptors.

Left: Soviet SAM-4 'Ganef' surface-to-air missiles on their tracked launchers. The SAM-4 has a maximum range of 70km, a minimum range of 9.3km and can reach up to an altitude of 25km. Many Soviet SAMs have been sold to countries throughout the Third World

In certain circumstances, the bludgeon of escorted strike may be preferable to the rapier of low-level evasion, as an attack force that has to evade enemy defences and to fight its way into the target area will find navigation and target acquisition all the more difficult. The ideal navigation system for an interdiction aircraft would be completely autonomous; that is, requiring no external data for position correction during the course of the flight. This would mean that the aircraft would make no EM emissions – which, as outlined earlier, are a potential means of detection and can provide an opportunity for jamming – and it would of course be thoroughly reliable. Modern electronic engineering has yet to produce such a system.

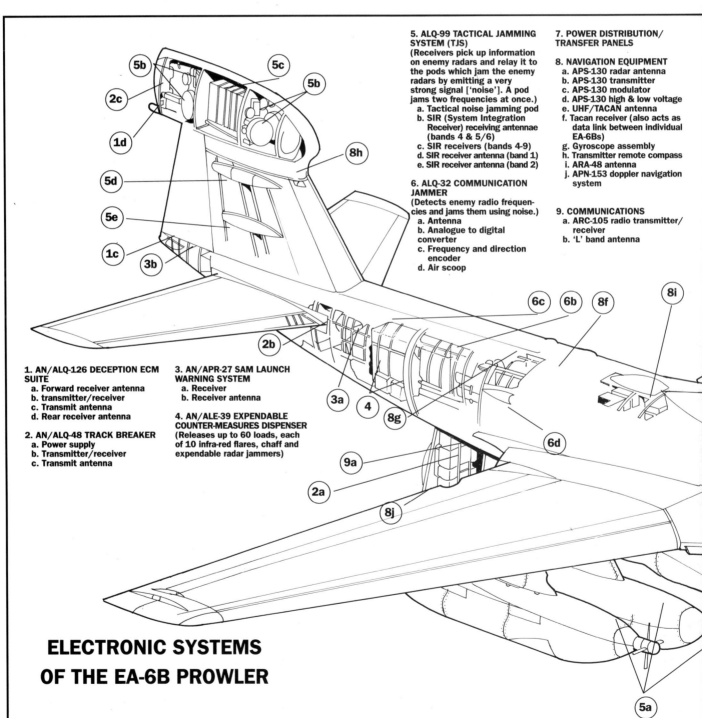

5. ALQ-99 TACTICAL JAMMING SYSTEM (TJS)
(Receivers pick up information on enemy radars and relay it to the pods which jam the enemy radars by emitting a very strong signal ['noise']. A pod jams two frequencies at once.)
a. Tactical noise jamming pod
b. SIR (System Integration Receiver) receiving antennae (bands 4 & 5/6)
c. SIR receivers (bands 4-9)
d. SIR receiver antenna (band 1)
e. SIR receiver antenna (band 2)

6. ALQ-32 COMMUNICATION JAMMER
(Detects enemy radio frequencies and jams them using noise.)
a. Antenna
b. Analogue to digital converter
c. Frequency and direction encoder
d. Air scoop

7. POWER DISTRIBUTION/ TRANSFER PANELS

8. NAVIGATION EQUIPMENT
a. APS-130 radar antenna
b. APS-130 transmitter
c. APS-130 modulator
d. APS-130 high & low voltage
e. UHF/TACAN antenna
f. Tacan receiver (also acts as data link between individual EA-6Bs)
g. Gyroscope assembly
h. Transmitter remote compass
i. ARA-48 antenna
j. APN-153 doppler navigation system

9. COMMUNICATIONS
a. ARC-105 radio transmitter/ receiver
b. 'L' band antenna

1. AN/ALQ-126 DECEPTION ECM SUITE
a. Forward receiver antenna
b. transmitter/receiver
c. Transmit antenna
d. Rear receiver antenna

2. AN/ALQ-48 TRACK BREAKER
a. Power supply
b. Transmitter/receiver
c. Transmit antenna

3. AN/APR-27 SAM LAUNCH WARNING SYSTEM
a. Receiver
b. Receiver antenna

4. AN/ALE-39 EXPENDABLE COUNTER-MEASURES DISPENSER
(Releases up to 60 loads, each of 10 infra-red flares, chaff and expendable radar jammers)

ELECTRONIC SYSTEMS OF THE EA-6B PROWLER

The Tornado interdiction/strike aircraft in service with the Royal Air Force, the German Luftwaffe and Italy's Aeronautica Militare relies on an inertial navigation system (INS) and a doppler velocity-sensing radar for its basic navigation information. The INS is autonomous in operation in the sense that it requires no external inputs, apart from feeding in the aircraft's precise position at the start of its flight.

The system, however, does suffer from 'slippage', and the accumulation of minor positional errors during the course of a two-hour sortie will create a significant circular error. For this reason, the Tornado crew must update the INS with position fixes during the flight. Typically, a series of prominent features (geographical or man-made) are selected as 'waypoints' along the pre-planned aircraft track. The navigator will pick them up on his radar and mark them by positioning a cursor over the waypoint's image on his radar screen, so correcting the flightpath. An experienced crew can do this very quickly indeed, but it does involve a telltale radar emission.

The Tornado crew must update the INS with fixes during the flight

The two separate sources of navigational data, the INS and the doppler, provide a cross-check on accuracy: a serious error in either system will immediately become apparent. However, the combined accuracy of the two is still insufficient for terrain-following flight. This calls for a specialised radar, which is of course another emitter, albeit one operating on a fairly narrow beam. Nevertheless, terrain-following by means of super-accurate navigation is certainly now within prospect. The system proposed for the Tornado's 'mid-life upgrade' will be verified by an apparatus similar to the cruise missile's terrain contour matching. This compares a radar image of the terrain below the aircraft with data stored in a navigation computer. Certainly the need for an emitter has not yet been entirely eliminated, but the new system won't be as easy to detect as terrain-following radar.

There can be no doubt that radar – used sparingly to avoid detection – will remain a valuable attack aircraft sensor for the foreseeable future. The USAF's new F-15E Strike Eagle, now coming into service to supplement the F-111 in the strike/interdiction role, has an especially valuable radar feature for target acquisition. Its AN/APG-70 radar can operate in a synthetic aperture mode for ground-mapping. This gives a high-resolution image of the target area after a few seconds' transmission. The image can then be 'frozen', allowing the radar to go onto standby if need be, while the aircraft's weapons system officer (WSO) sets up the attack using the stored radar data.

The need for an emitter has not yet been entirely eliminated

Synthetic aperture techniques, hitherto used for reconnaissance rather than attack radars, obtain an extremely detailed radar picture by electronically 'enlarging' the aerial, the physical dimensions of which are severely restricted by the limited space available on the aircraft. The F-15E also uses the pod-mounted LANTIRN system, which provides FLIR imagery for both navigation and attack. The main radar retains an air-to-air capability and so, unlike most interdiction aircraft, the F-15E can transform itself from an attack aircraft into an air superiority fighter.

FLIRs and laser rangefinders are extremely useful in target acquisition and weapons delivery. The USAF's F-111F's WSO can use the aircraft's Pave Tack system to acquire his target using FLIR and

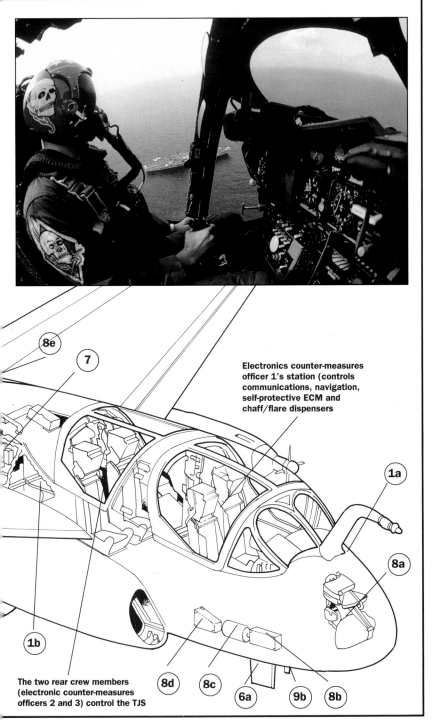

Electronics counter-measures officer 1's station (controls communications, navigation, self-protective ECM and chaff/flare dispensers)

The two rear crew members (electronic counter-measures officers 2 and 3) control the TJS

INVISIBLE AIRCRAFT
STEALTH TECHNOLOGY EXPLAINED

The next generation of tactical aircraft will all have some level of 'stealth' technology to improve their chances of survival in combat and against air defences. Various techniques will reduce the radar cross-section, infra-red, visual – and perhaps aural – signatures of aircraft to the point where they will no longer give the enemy an early enough warning of their approach or a sufficiently reliable means of target tracking and weapons guidance.

A 'stealthy' aircraft will also need to reduce or entirely eliminate its own electromagnetic emissions. These are essentially the aims of Stealth programmes. The idea that stealth technology makes an aircraft literally invisible is really journalistic hyperbole; the objective in the design of a high-performance fighter is rather to ensure that its pilot can pick up an enemy and then laser-designate it for attack by his own or an

launch a missile against it before the target is aware of the danger.

The first Stealth aircraft, the US Air Force's Lockheed F-117A and Northrop B-2, largely rely on their much reduced radar signatures to allow them to penetrate defended airspace. The coming generation is likely to combine 'stealthiness' with other aids to penetration, such as a high service ceiling, agility and speed. Thus an interdiction aircraft such as the American A-12/ Advanced Tactical Aircraft will be able to operate again in the high- and medium-altitude bands that SAMs and interceptors have for long denied to unescorted strike aircraft. However, the US believes that Soviet aircraft designers will produce successors to the Su-27 Flanker and MiG-29 Fulcrum for service in the next century, so perhaps the ATF will not be entirely in a class of its own.

---

accompanying aircraft; alternatively, he can use Pave Tack to determine the range by laser range finder. The accuracy with which weapons can be delivered has also been improved by increased computer capacity. For example, one RAF Tornado GR Mk 1 can deliver 'dumb' bombs with greater accuracy in a loft-bombing attack than its predecessor the Jaguar can achieve using laydown bombing.

In view of the tremendous improvements in attack aircraft since World War II, it is astounding that the weapons these aircraft will deliver on the majority of their sorties are freefall bombs no different in concept from the bombs dropped in that conflict. This phenomenon can be explained in part by the philosophy that it is better, and cheaper, to build sophisticated guidance into the aircraft – which (it is hoped) will return – rather than into the weapon, which will be expended. The other major inhibiting factor in air-weapon development has been a simple lack of adequate funding; aircraft development tends to absorb the lion's share of an air force's research-and-development budget.

Specialised bombs are available for many different purposes

There can be little doubt that this situation will change over the coming decade. Not only will increasingly effective air defence threats put a premium on long-range stand-off weapons, but budgets for new aircraft procurement are likely to drop. The latter will mean extending the life of aircraft currently in service, and developing and fitting more effective weaponry will be a good way of achieving this. The French Armee de l'Air has extended the useful life of its Mirage IVs long beyond their 'natural' span largely through fitting them with the ASMP stand-off missile.

The type of target to be attacked decides the sort of bomb that will be used against it. If the

bomb is to penetrate concrete – in an attack on a runway or hardened aircraft shelter, for example – the variables to consider include the depth and the quality of the concrete, the strength and shape of the bomb casing and the bomb's angle of impact. The need to operate at low level can complicate the problems of bomb design, as the weapon then needs to be retarded – that is, slowed down in flight – typically by extending braking vanes, as in the American Snakeye. This lets the aircraft escape the blast and fragmentation of its own bombs during laydown at low altitude.

New bombing techniques have been developed for new bombs

However, retarding the bomb reduces its velocity at impact and the steepness of its angle of impact, and thus its penetrative ability. Ideally, the bomb should be released at a comparatively high altitude and at an angle near to the vertical in order to obtain the optimum result against a hardened structure. This is how laydown bombing works, but the bomber must fly at altitude in order to make the weapons effective. To achieve this and yet allow the aircraft to fly at low level for protection, the loft-bombing method has been developed. This involves the aircraft approaching at low level and then climbing sharply and at speed some way short of the target, when the bomb is released and tossed on to the target following a parabolic trajectory. The technique is less accurate than laydown, however, and is therefore more effective against larger, fixed targets. But if the requirement is for surface blast (to wreck buildings, aircraft or vehicles) or fragmentation (to kill people), retarded bombs are perfectly adequate, and have the great advantage of being directly aimed from an aircraft which has not exposed itself to ground fire.

Cluster bombs extend the weapon's area of effective coverage and compensate in some degree

Above: Lockheed's F-117A Stealth fighter is probably the most radical development in aviation since the jet engine. The first generation flew in 1977, but it wasn't until 12 years later that one was used operationally, during Operation Just Cause, the invasion of Panama. The aircraft's relatively low maximum speed – just over 1000km/h – is a by-product of airframe design. The next generation can be expected to be considerably faster

for inaccuracies in delivery. These can be composed of anti-personnel or anti-tank bomblets, which are dispersed in a pattern, typically doughnut shaped, to cover a wide area. As with conventional bombs, they can be delivered either in laydown or loft manoeuvres. Unguided rockets fired in salvoes will also destroy anything in their way over a fairly wide area, but have largely gone out of fashion, due to their inherent inaccuracy.

The natural extension of the cluster bomb principle is the weapons dispenser, which releases bomblets directly from the aircraft rather than from a cluster bomb as it falls earthwards. Dispensers can carry a large load of bomblets and so are well suited to airfield attack or for dealing with large armoured concentrations. However, it does require the aircraft to overfly the target and for this reason alone the bomblet dispenser will probably not have much of a future beyond the present generation MW-1, used by the Luftwaffe, and the RAF's JP 233. Laser-guided bombs offer a new dimension in accuracy, but demand that the target be illuminated

STEALTH TECHNOLOGY OF THE F-117A

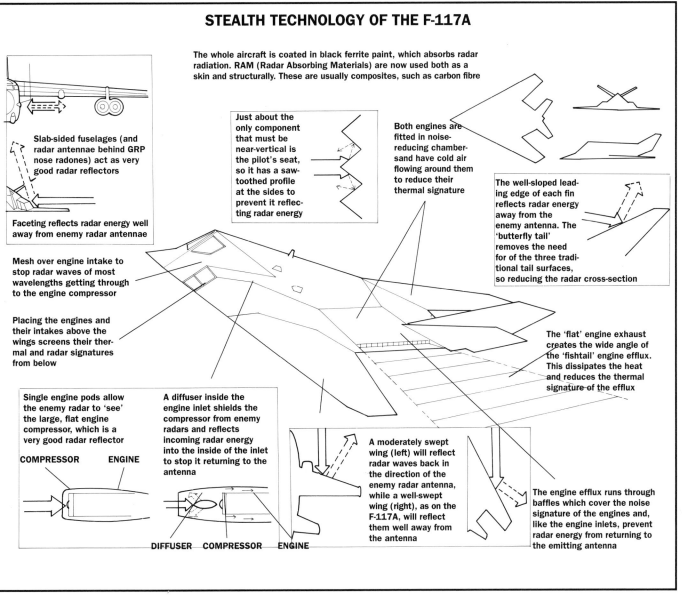

The whole aircraft is coated in black ferrite paint, which absorbs radar radiation. RAM (Radar Absorbing Materials) are now used both as a skin and structurally. These are usually composites, such as carbon fibre

Slab-sided fuselages (and radar antennae behind GRP nose radomes) act as very good radar reflectors

Faceting reflects radar energy well away from enemy radar antennae

Mesh over engine intake to stop radar waves of most wavelengths getting through to the engine compressor

Placing the engines and their intakes above the wings screens their thermal and radar signatures from below

Single engine pods allow the enemy radar to 'see' the large, flat engine compressor, which is a very good radar reflector

COMPRESSOR   ENGINE

A diffuser inside the engine inlet shields the compressor from enemy radars and reflects incoming radar energy into the inside of the inlet to stop it returning to the antenna

DIFFUSER   COMPRESSOR   ENGINE

Just about the only component that must be near-vertical is the pilot's seat, so it has a saw-toothed profile at the sides to prevent it reflecting radar energy

Both engines are fitted in noise-reducing chamber-sand have cold air flowing around them to reduce their thermal signature

The well-sloped leading edge of each fin reflects radar energy away from the enemy antenna. The 'butterfly tail' removes the need for of the three traditional tail surfaces, so reducing the radar cross-section

The 'flat' engine exhaust creates the wide angle of the 'fishtail' engine efflux. This dissipates the heat and reduces the thermal signature of the efflux

A moderately swept wing (left) will reflect radar waves back in the direction of the enemy radar antenna, while a well-swept wing (right), as on the F-117A, will reflect them well away from the antenna

The engine efflux runs through baffles which cover the noise signature of the engines and, like the engine inlets, prevent radar energy from returning to the emitting antenna

throughout the bomb's flight, by the releasing aircraft's laser designator, by an accompanying aircraft, or from a ground position within line-of-sight of the desired impact point.

Stand-off weapons (either missiles or unpowered glide bombs), minimise the launch aircraft's exposure to the target's point air defence, but at the price of making target acquisition much more difficult. Not all targets will be fixed in one position, and so the use of stand-off weapons presupposes the availability firstly of near-real time reconnaissance information and secondly of a weapons-guidance system that is able to recognise its target. A TV or imaging-infra-red guidance system, such as that on the American AGM-65 Maverick series, is one option; another is laser guidance. Millimetric radar seekers may prove useful for future air-to-surface missiles.

Unguided rockets fired in salvoes will destroy anything in their way

A formation attack helps solve the problem of how to hit the target and at the same time avoid exposure to air defences. A group of aircraft can provide a degree of mutual support against fighter attack, and a synchronised approach to the target from various headings will dissipate the concentration of defensive fire. Yet mass attacks have their problems. They call for accurate timing and co-ordination between individual aircraft, which must usually observe radio silence at the same time. For example, if following aircraft are not to run into the blast of the preceding aircraft's weapons and if collisions are to be avoided, each bomb run must be separated by a few seconds, yet too great a gap between attack runs will simply allow the defenders to deal with the attacking aircraft one by one.

Another disadvantage of attacking in formation is that the smoke and debris from the initial attack runs will also tend to obscure aiming points for the following aircraft. This could well render electro-optically guided weapons ineffective, although free-fall bombs could be dropped blind if the pilot starts his bombing run from a predetermined point at a known distance from the target and precisely times the moment when he releases the weapon. Wind direction could therefore be significant in determining the direction from which he approaches the target, but the pilot would also balance other tactical considerations against the need to avoid the worst effects of smoke.

Smoke and debris from initial attacks will obscure later aiming

Many factors will lessen or increase the overall effectiveness and reliability of interdiction bombing. Weather conditions and hours of daylight, for example, could well affect accuracy, with the lower incidence of cloud and longer daylight hours of the summer months offering obvious advantages. The effectiveness and density of enemy air defences will dictate how far interdictors can penetrate his airspace. Also significant to the success of a mission will be the level of sophistication of the attacking aircraft, and of the weapons it carries.

Stand-off and precision-guided munitions will probably be in relatively short supply (if only because of their sheer expense) and are therefore likely to be set aside for use against the most difficult targets. Similarly, the most advanced aircraft will be carefully matched against the most demanding missions and some may well be held back from a conventional bombing campaign as a tactical nuclear delivery force. Even with an attrition rate of one per cent per sortie (and figures of around 10 per cent were nearer the norm during periods of heavy fighting in World War II), losses will soon mount.

Assuming that aircraft fly an average of 2.8 sorties per day, a one per cent attrition rate will reduce them by half over a 24-day period of continuous operations. Battle damage to aircraft, crew

Right: A Stinger surface-to-air missile destroys a QF-106 target drone. The Stinger is a shoulder-launched weapon that homes in on the heat emissions from the aircraft – both from its engines and from the friction generated by its flight through the air. While the Stinger is relatively difficult to jam, earlier types of shoulder-launched, infra-red homing missiles are easily decoyed by dropping flares. In the 1973 Arab-Israeli War, for instance, of the 4356 Soviet-supplied SAM-7s that were launched, only 34 hit their targets

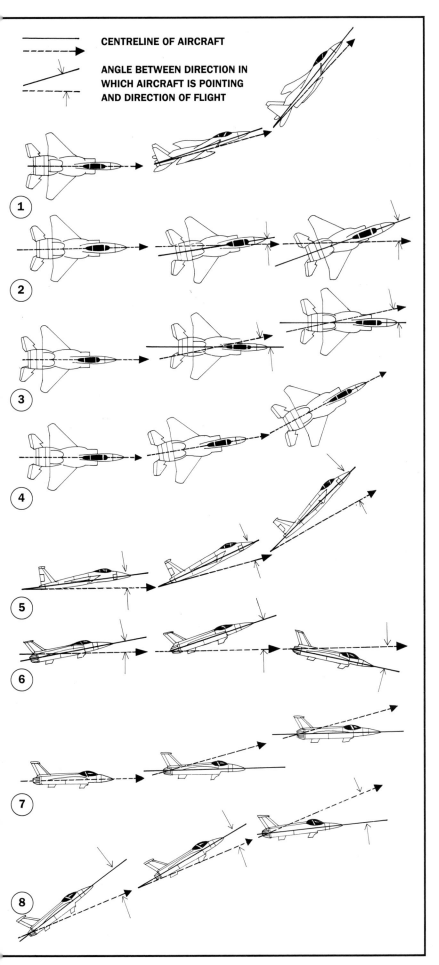

CENTRELINE OF AIRCRAFT

ANGLE BETWEEN DIRECTION IN WHICH AIRCRAFT IS POINTING AND DIRECTION OF FLIGHT

exhaustion and combat stress, together with the depletion of munitions stocks will all lead to diminishing returns from the surviving force as the campaign progresses. Target planning will therefore be at a premium, with the likely effect of any mission on the enemy to be carefully weighed against the price that his defences will exact.

There are some, however, who would argue that the day of the manned aircraft is fast drawing to a close, at least as a direct support weapon of the land armies.

Precision-guided munitions will be in relatively short supply

They point to the increasing vulnerability of manned aircraft over the battlefield, to the high cost of procuring and operating them and to the additional expense of providing highly trained air and ground crews. There is little, argue the proponents of unmanned aerial vehicles (UAVs – drones and remotely piloted vehicles, or RPVs), to be lost by taking the pilot 'out of the loop', and much to be gained. Airmen hotly contest this view, pointing out that a switch to UAVs would mean the loss of air power's much-prized ability to react to the unexpected when it occurs. Moreover, although RPVs are cheaper and can be fielded in greater numbers than manned aircraft, their loss rate from enemy action and accident is expected to be much higher. Complex and vulnerable communications links from air to ground will be needed to operate RPVs, while drones will need to be pre-programmed and thus will lose all flexibility.

Even with an attrition rate of one per cent, losses will soon mount

The Israeli experience in the Beqaa Valley in 1982 suggests that drones have a useful part to play alongside manned aircraft. This is a valuable lesson that is likely to be blurred in the present debate on manned versus unmanned aircraft as the various services fight for their interests. One of the attractions of drones and RPVs for the army commander is that he can operate them himself, while the air forces are, for obvious emotional reasons, aghast at the idea of replacing their fighter and attack aircraft with UAVs. The air forces' resistance to UAVs is likely to transcend that of the horse cavalry regiments to mechanisation in the 1920s and 1930s, though in its support, one should perhaps say that the case for the manned aircraft is intrinsically more sound than that for the 'well-bred horse'.

But there's more to air power than strike missions. Aerial reconnaissance is vitally important to the land commander, and its value is usually in direct proportion to its timeliness; hence the emphasis in modern reconnaissance systems on the 'real-time' transmission of data, which may be gathered either by optical sensors or in other parts of electromagnetic spectrum. The fighters' battle for air superiority is another area in which air power will decisively influence what happens on the ground. It is an area which has consistently been undervalued by

Left: It costs in excess of a million pounds to train a fast-mover pilot, who might have a life expectancy measured in days, in the event of war. This A-10 pilot, who has no air-to-air combat training (and lacks even rudimentary air-to-air combat weapons systems in his aircraft), has to absorb a different set of skills, which include feature and vehicle recognition and low flying.
Below: An F-14 Tomcat on the Grumman production line, giving an idea of the complexity of modern combat aircraft that makes them so expensive. Some of the systems are there purely because it is a manned aircraft. Having an unmanned aircraft makes it smaller and more capable, as machines can withstand stresses and manoeuvres beyond the physical limits of a human being

land commanders. This is well illustrated by the classic 1970s story in which two victorious Soviet tank army commanders meet on the banks of the Rhine and one is asked by the other, 'And who was it that won the air battle?' In real warfare, the answer to this question would be all too evident, since on the outcome of the fight for air superiority depends the freedom of one's own ground forces to operate without undue interference from enemy air power and also the ability of friendly tactical air forces to intervene directly in the ground fighting.

Fixed-wing transport aircraft can also deploy airborne forces

Finally, we come to air transport operations. Their role is significant in that it affects the speed at which ground forces can be deployed, reinforced and resupplied. Neither fixed-wing transport aircraft nor utility and heavy-lift helicopters will be able to move more than a small proportion of ground troops (and even less of their equipment), but nonetheless, airlift's ability to transport reinforcements into the theatre of operations at great speed is likely to play an important part in the opening moves of the battle. Similarly, the helicopter's ability to reinforce any part of the battlefield rapidly confers great tactical

DOES THE MANNED BOMBER HAVE A FUTURE?

Those who say that the manned bomber has a bright future, despite the threat from ET weapons, argue as follows:

• Stealth technology and other counter-measures give it unprecedented protection and make successfully completed missions far more likely

• Unmanned ET interdiction systems such as strike drones and 'smart' missiles are still untested in battle. The manned bomber, however, is a well-tried and tested tool for the same job

• Smart and brilliant weapon stores now allow a single bomber to fly missions that once would have required many aircraft

• Unlike a pre-programmed drone or missile, the manned bomber can attack targets of opportunity

• The manned bomber can be flown over and over again, whereas existing unmanned systems are regarded as disposable. The more missions a bomber can complete, the better value for money it gives. Unmanned weapons can be used only once – and consequently their final costs in terms of 'bang per buck' will be higher in a protracted war

The arguments against are:

• New and emerging missiles may be able to defeat the bomber's counter-measures

• Unmanned ET weapons may cost less in the long run than manned bombers if

bomber combat losses prove to be high – and ET weapons do not put pilots at risk

• New weapons will make airfields unusable, both by destroying runways and making repair impossible with chemical weapons

advantages on the army which is trained and prepared to use this asset with flair and imagination.

However, the Boeing CH-47 Chinook, the largest helicopter in use by NATO, can carry only 12 tons of cargo at the very most, and is a sitting duck to the new generation of SAM and anti-aircraft fire and even the most rudimentary form of air-to-air attack. Tactical heavy-lift helicopters, therefore, have to rely on their lighter, more agile and more heavily armed colleagues to keep them alive.

Fixed-wing transport aircraft can also deploy airborne forces, and 'special forces' will require both fixed-wing and rotary-wing airlift. The USAF and US Army have assigned dedicated air units to the support of their Special Forces troops – which is not only indicative of the importance that the United States accords to such forces, but also recognises one of the principal failings of air transport. Namely, that it will always be in short supply and that many difficult decisions will have to be made between conflicting claims on its services – all of which are likely to have strong arguments in their favour. US Special Forces at least do not have to get involved in those arguments – although the debate about the 'correct' tactical and strategic uses of air power will doubtless continue for as long as aircraft, manned or not, go to war.

Above: Computer-aided design of the YF-23, one of the contenders for the USAF ATF (Advanced Tactical Fighter) competition. It remains to be seen if the ATF's successor will be unmanned, or whether the ATF will be amongst the last generation of manned aircraft

IS THE TANK DEAD?

In 1939, the German army astonished the world with the speed and efficiency with which its armoured columns over-ran vast tracts of Europe. In fact the success of those early advances probably owed more to other factors than to the tanks themselves. One was the brilliance of the German concept of *blitzkrieg* itself. The other stemmed from the opposing armies' disregard for the tank and for mobile armoured warfare. They failed to develop an anti-tank doctrine or to equip themselves properly. The lesson, however, has been well learned. Since the 1940s an 'extended family' of anti-tank weapons has appeared, and ever more complex and far-fetched systems are constantly being added to it.

At first sight, modern developments could suggest that contemporary tanks would be destroyed almost as soon as they appear, and that battles will in future have to be based upon completely different types of weapons systems. However, the tank itself is now enormously more sophisticated than it was in 1939 – with the introduction of much-improved passive armour, reactive armour and active counter-measures; not to mention increased horse-power, electronic power and firepower. The tank can now move faster and hit harder than ever; it can see in the dark; and – perhaps most important – it can fight off most incoming warheads with a wide variety of self-defence mechanisms. Stealth technology for tanks, comparable to that used in the B2 bomber aircraft, is already being developed.

The tank can now move faster and hit harder than ever

All this means that we do not really know which currently has the edge: the tank or the anti-tank measures. Thus it may be true that the tank is finally dead, as lobbyists for the new AT weaponry continue to insist. Equally, it may be true that the armour lobby is right to claim that the tank is only just beginning a new lease of life. Both sides seem to have a case: in the 1973 October War between Israel and Egypt and Syria, and the 1980-89 Gulf War, most tank attacks were quickly stopped in their tracks, while in the 1982 invasion of Lebanon the tank was

LEFT: The detonation of the 155 mm HEAT (High Explosive Anti-Tank) warhead of a Copperhead CLGP (Cannon-Launched Guided Projectile). It has hit the side of an obsolete M47 medium tank being used as a range target. This photograph shows how the HEAT warhead explodes in every direction, though only that part of the explosion directed towards the tank is used to penetrate the target's armour. Today's main battle tanks are often fitted with reactive or composite armour which greatly reduce the penetrating power of even such large-calibre HEAT warheads

ARMOUR PROTECTION OF A MODERN MAIN BATTLE TANK

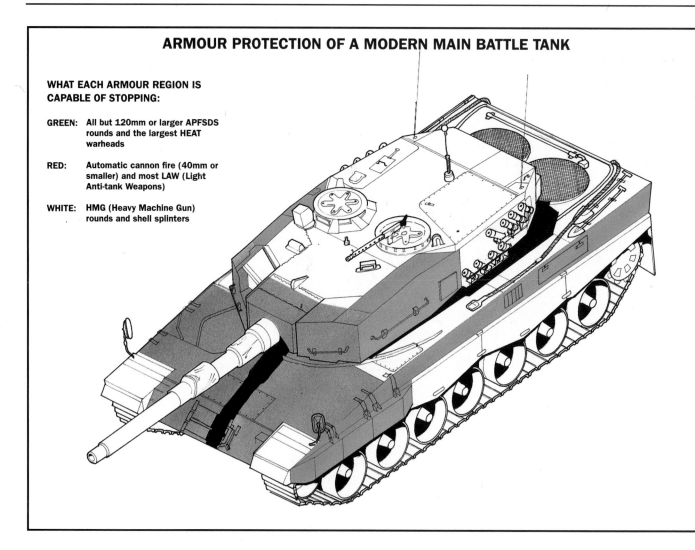

WHAT EACH ARMOUR REGION IS CAPABLE OF STOPPING:

GREEN: All but 120mm or larger APFSDS rounds and the largest HEAT warheads

RED: Automatic cannon fire (40mm or smaller) and most LAW (Light Anti-tank Weapons)

WHITE: HMG (Heavy Machine Gun) rounds and shell splinters

still able to fight its way forward despite taking heavy losses from infantry anti-tank weapons.

There is no doubt that the tank is vulnerable to an enormous range of weapons; not solely to those dedicated to AT duties. Straightforward primitive weapons have always posed a certain threat – for example the Madrid dynamiters of 1936 or the 1945 Japanese officers who occasionally got inside British tanks in Burma with their slashing swords. Equally, simple obstacles placed on the battlefield by engineers can exert an important channelling effect, as did the anti-tank ditches on the Golan in 1973. Even snipers armed with rifles are still lethal since, despite modern optics and communications, tank commanders still tend to operate best with

their hatches open and heads up. Then there are tank-killing infantry teams, which may infiltrate into leaguer areas to cause havoc among crews performing maintenance or replenishment work. Conventional artillery can also make its mark, with HE shelling seemingly much more damaging to tanks today than it was in the past, as a result of greatly improved accuracy, fragmentation and sheer blast power. The last-mentioned is useful in disrupting the array of sensitive sensors and antennae on a tank's exterior.

Modern armies field a wide range of relatively light (that is, between 75mm and 90mm) anti-armour guns that are designated for use against APCs but which, if they can achieve a lucky hit on

Above: Vickers Medium and Light tanks of the British Army in training between WWI and WWII. Many pundits in the inter-war years said that the tank had had its day, because of the anti-tank gun

Right: Soviet T-55 tanks ford a river during an exercise. More of this type of tank have been produced than any other in history

Left: The Swedish turretless Strv-103 S-Tank. Hailed as revolutionary when it first appeared in 1966, the S-Tank has a 105mm gun which is fixed in the hull. The gun is traversed by turning the whole tank using the tracks, and it is elevated and depressed by raising or lowering the forward or rear part of the hydropneumatic suspension. This means that the S-tank cannot track targets, or fire, on the move – a tactical handicap. It is very effective in defence as a tank destroyer, in the manner of the German 'SP guns' of World War II. The S-Tank has a very low silhouette, good protection for the crew and ammunition, and a high rate of fire

One battalion per kilometre – a tank every 40 metres of front – at first sight looks like an awful lot of tanks, but on the ground each battalion commander would be very conscious of how limited his force actually was. Advancing into an enemy-held locality, he – and his crews – would want to go slowly and cautiously, only too well aware of how quickly his force could be reduced to a mere handful. A unit commander would know that a hidden and waiting enemy holds many advantages over a moving unit, so he would try to leapfrog forward in short bounds, consolidating each new position in turn. Every movement would be overwatched by tanks ready to fire as soon as the enemy revealed himself – and those tanks in turn would be overwatched by air-defence guns and missiles. Infantry or fire would have to check out every potentially threatening piece of cover along the way – which artillery would perhaps smoke off while the tanks manoeuvred past it. Every potential minefield or patch of boggy ground would have to be skirted. Reconnaissance units would probe forward, flanks would be watched for any attempt at penetration.

This type of all-arms battle can quickly become very complex, needing especially efficient communications if the commander is to retain control. All too easily he can find sub-units becoming detached or getting involved in small local combats of their own, spreading out laterally as well as in depth – so diluting the spearhead and using up the

force. In this way, all too quickly, the 'battalion concentrated on a kilometre of front' can melt away to an isolated troop fighting on its own.

The tactics for individual tanks are based on the principle of maintaining maximum concealment up to – and even during – the moment of opening fire. Where possible tanks will take position behind a ridge or in scrapes which can be dug in less than an hour by modern earth-moving plant. Defilade positions are preferred so that the enemy can be engaged from a concealed position on his flank. If there is time, the tank crew will camouflage the vehicle and, where appropriate, lay out dummy positions and decoy heat sources to divert enemy surveillance and fire.

Where possible, tanks will take position behind a ridge or scrape

When waiting to make contact with the enemy, tanks may be turret down – that is, showing only the commander's cupola above ground level; then to fire they may come hull down – showing only the turret. During the engagement, they may put down suppressive fire – terrorising the enemy, in short – with their machine guns, as well as firing their main guns, and employ a variety of ECMs, such as flares to decoy heat-seeking warheads. Once they have fired, the tanks may revert to their concealed positions or – preferably, in view of the threat from both direct and indirect fire – move to an altogether new position. If they are caught in the open, they can lay down a screen of smoke and hastily retreat to the nearest cover. Despite the risk of throwing a track, modern tanks will use surges of power for short sprints at high speed from one piece of cover to another; the American M1 and Soviet T80 can both manage up to 70km/h on a good surface.

Life in a tank is not as easy as the infantry might like to imagine. It is cramped – especially in Soviet main battle tanks (MBTs), which are much smaller than their Western counterparts – and very bumpy when travelling at speed. There are many hard objects inside a tank: broken noses are an occupational hazard among tank crews. Needing to know what is going on outside only makes life harder. Even with modern all-round optics, the commander has difficulty seeing what he needs to see unless he opens his hatch (a move that can be fatal), while the remainder of the turret crew can see next to nothing of what is going on. The driver has a better view to the outside if the commander has 'buttoned up'. But it is a very restricted view, and he is isolated from his comrades in a lonely station in the front of the hull, from which, in many tanks, he cannot escape as long as the main gun is facing forward. In fact, evacuating the tank quickly in an emergency is difficult for everyone. Smoke, fire and especially explosion are the main enemies of tank crews, although the Israelis have pioneered innovative fire-suppression systems, which use halon gas to starve the flames of oxygen, with considerable success in their Merkava tank. The American Abrams M1 and German Leopard 2 tanks now use the same means to control internal fires.

Smoke, fire and explosion are the main enemies of tank crews

Manning a tank demands split-second decision-making from all crew members. The commander must communicate with other tanks, while selecting targets and designating them to his own crew; the gunner must see and lay on to these targets quickly; and the driver must keep the vehicle positioned to optimum effect. On the modern battlefield these life-and-death decisions will need to be made faster than ever, and more complex equipment – such as apparatus to control the tank's main armament, ECMs and camouflage – will be involved than ever. In the stress and fatigue of battle, a moment's inattention may break any link in this complex chain, possibly with disastrous results.

And there are many disasters that may befall an inattentive tank crew or tank unit. The fate of the 4th County of London Yeomanry at Villers Bocage, Normandy, 1944, is eloquent. A column of its Cromwells and Sherman Fireflies, along with a company from the Rifle Brigade in Universal Carriers and half-tracks, were caught without flank protection while lined up along a narrow road, so just three German Tiger tanks were able to destroy them, vehicle by vehicle. On the modern battlefield a much greater number of such incidents may be expected to take place – and tanks will not be at

PROTECTIVE MEASURES OF THE A-10A THUNDERBOLT II

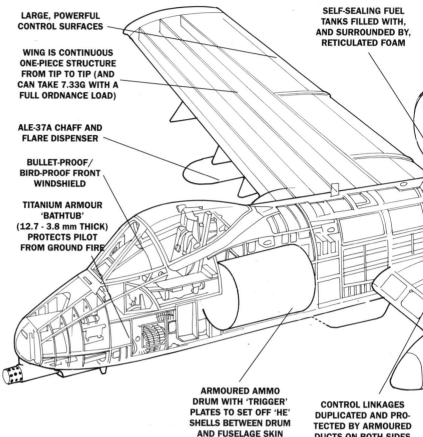

LARGE, POWERFUL CONTROL SURFACES

WING IS CONTINUOUS ONE-PIECE STRUCTURE FROM TIP TO TIP (AND CAN TAKE 7.33G WITH A FULL ORDNANCE LOAD)

ALE-37A CHAFF AND FLARE DISPENSER

BULLET-PROOF/ BIRD-PROOF FRONT WINDSHIELD

TITANIUM ARMOUR 'BATHTUB' (12.7 - 3.8 mm THICK) PROTECTS PILOT FROM GROUND FIRE

SELF-SEALING FUEL TANKS FILLED WITH, AND SURROUNDED BY, RETICULATED FOAM

ARMOURED AMMO DRUM WITH 'TRIGGER' PLATES TO SET OFF 'HE' SHELLS BETWEEN DRUM AND FUSELAGE SKIN

CONTROL LINKAGES DUPLICATED AND PROTECTED BY ARMOURED DUCTS ON BOTH SIDES OF AIRCRAFT (A-10 ALSO USES CABLES RATHER THAN RODS, AS THEY ARE LESS LIKELY TO JAM AFTER BATTLE DAMAGE

OTHER POINTS:
1. The interchangeability of many port and starboard components of the aircraft reduces the number of spares needed
2. Most of the skin area of the aircraft is unstressed, which simplifies the repair task

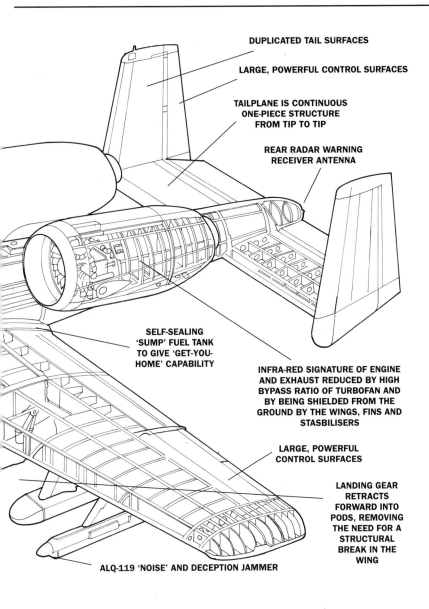

DUPLICATED TAIL SURFACES

LARGE, POWERFUL CONTROL SURFACES

TAILPLANE IS CONTINUOUS ONE-PIECE STRUCTURE FROM TIP TO TIP

REAR RADAR WARNING RECEIVER ANTENNA

SELF-SEALING 'SUMP' FUEL TANK TO GIVE 'GET-YOU-HOME' CAPABILITY

INFRA-RED SIGNATURE OF ENGINE AND EXHAUST REDUCED BY HIGH BYPASS RATIO OF TURBOFAN AND BY BEING SHIELDED FROM THE GROUND BY THE WINGS, FINS AND STASBILISERS

LARGE, POWERFUL CONTROL SURFACES

LANDING GEAR RETRACTS FORWARD INTO PODS, REMOVING THE NEED FOR A STRUCTURAL BREAK IN THE WING

ALQ-119 'NOISE' AND DECEPTION JAMMER

risk merely from enemy armour, but from the whole range of new indirect-fire weapons as well.

Nor has the sheer physical toil facing tank crews been abolished by such ostensibly labour-saving features as bagged charges and other 'separate' ammunition or automated ammunition handling. Crews still have to tension tracks on most tanks, and have to service engines; to bring ammunition aboard and manhandle camouflage nets. Merely mounting and dismounting these giant 60-ton monsters is something of an athletic feat in itself. Admittedly mechanical digging equipment can now help add protection to a static position, but in general a tank's crew gets precious little help from outside. It is a distinct unit that must fend for itself, 24 hours a day.

The very size of the tank makes for hard work

The main threat to combat efficiency, however, may well rest not with stress, physical fatigue, or new weapons, but with the very ancient problem of making a successful rendezvous (RV). It has always been notoriously difficult for commanders to manoeuvre their own forces, and for troops to navigate their way, to a particular spot to arrive at a particular moment, especially through terrain with restricted lines of sight, such as forest or mountain country. When two separate forces are both trying to reach the same RV at the same time, the problem becomes more than twice as difficult to overcome. New, satellite-based navigation aids may tell units exactly where they are and where they have to be, but they do not necessarily speed their progress. An infantry force travelling by truck may be tied to roads that have been interdicted by the enemy, whereas tanks can crash across country: whichever makes the deadline first will be exposed to attack while it waits for the other. Making these manoeuvres work requires a

Left: Rearming the 30mm GAU-8/A 'Avenger' cannon on an A-10A. Built specifically as a tank-busting aircraft – with the cannon as its main anti-armour weapon – the Thunderbolt II follows the WWI Junkers J1 and the WWII Il-2 Sturmvoik in being heavily armoured itself

Right: The awesome firepower of a GAU-8. This weapon can fire at 2100 or 4200 rpm, but to prevent overheating the 1174 rounds the A-10A carries are fired in 10 two-second bursts

Right: US Marines firing a SMAW (Shoulder-launched Multi-purpose Assault Weapon) at a T-72 tank. The SMAW is a modification of the Israeli B-300 82mm anti-armour weapon. Because of the small size of the warhead, it can only penetrate 400mm of rolled homogenous steel armour, which means that it has to be fired against the side of a modern main battle tank, rather than the front, to be effective. But against more lightly armoured targets – such as APCs and IFVs (Infantry Fighting Vehicles), such weapons are devastating

high level of 'staff work' – often from very junior commanders or even individual vehicle crews. As the speed of operations increases, so does the number of RVs that are needed. The schedules become tighter and the possibility of failure increases.

There is probably nothing in land warfare more difficult than orchestrating an impromptu, fast-moving armoured battle fought by small sub-units. In World War II only a few commanders – for example, O'Connor (whose motto was 'offensive action whenever possible', but whose potential was cut short when he was captured), Rommel, Von Balck and Patton – could ride this particular bronco for very long, and Patton often did so only by bypassing and so isolating heavy concentrations of enemy units. The general consensus was that it was always safer to plan for a deliberate, slow-moving, attritional battle in which massive force could be remorselessly lined up against identified enemy weak points and, in the end, the Allies' greater industrial resources justified this stand. Montgomery, for all his bluster about chasing the enemy 'like a frightened rabbit', stuck firmly to this strategy both in North Africa and in the European theatre. This sedate and resource-intensive style did ultimately win the war – but the whole thing might have been a shorter and less bloody business had the Allied high command had the talent available to follow, or had encouraged, a more swashbuckling approach.

Opportunistic attacks, brilliant improvisation and lightning responses may be the only way to win a future war. But such a fighting style presumes that supplies will always be available on demand to continue the battle, to exploit advantages or recoup losses. On the battlefield of the future, there is no problem that will be more acute than logistics.

Heavily armoured columns must fight an unpredictable battle of wide-ranging manoeuvre, then link up almost instantly – still somewhere not far away from the battlefield – with their soft-skinned supply echelons. The rate at which modern armour will consume ammunition makes this a crucial matter. Making it succeed will make heavy work for combat and staff troops alike: for the armoured troops there are all the difficulties of disengaging from the fighting and moving to find a particular – and reasonably safe – spot in the rear; for the logisticians there is the hardly less daunting task of predicting where the 'tankies' will want to be, and when.

Tanks can be as vulnerable as any soft-skinned vehicle

We may well be entering an era in which armoured vehicles will have to carry out all logistic replenishment, since the present soft-skinned ones will be unable to survive in the places where tanks must resupply. But even this provision may not be enough, for while tanks and heavily armoured vehicles may be becoming proof against hand-held infantry weapons, they can be as vulnerable as any soft-skinned vehicle to almost any other type of weapon if they are caught off guard. Furthermore, the appearance of effective indirect-fire anti-armour weapons, in particular, has now abolished the tank's traditional safety outside the enemy's line of sight. The tank's freedom of action is today being restricted from many directions at once, and it is unlikely to dominate the battlefield of the future in the same way that it dominated the battlefield in the past. The tank may not be dead, but from now on it will have to be more wary than ever.

IS THE TANK DEAD?

Some answer this question with an unequivocal 'yes'. Their reasons:

• The tank now faces a bewildering range of anti-tank weapons, and many, many more of them it ever faced before. As well as direct-fire weapons there are tube artillery-launched scattered field mines, smart 'search-and-destroy armour' mines and self-forging projectiles that hang beneath parachutes, waiting for a target to appear below them

• Thermal imagery and other new surveillance devices highlight tanks when they move, although they can be defeated by tanks lurking in ambush. This reverses the traditional offensive role of the tank

• Other classes of AFV – for example, SPGs, armoured cars and attack helicopters – may take over the tank's role

• The complex all-arms battle that the tank

demands will be very hard to fight if tactical communications are lost and logistics are uncertain

Others disagree. Their reasons:

• Many new AT weapons are expensive, complicated, and little tested in combat. Even if enough of them can be put into the field, it is uncertain that they will work properly

• New passive, reactive and perhaps even active armour, ECMs and fire suppression systems make the tank safer than ever, especially against portable HEAT weapons

• The heavy KE gun will be the best AT weapon, and only another tank can carry it. If the electro-magnetic rail gun can be fielded, this will be more true than ever

• Modern all-arms teams contain a mix of powerful AFVs and other kit that is better designed for the integrated battle than ever

US operation in Grenada, where rotary-wing losses were relatively high.

Also very worrying to helicopters is the likelihood that enemy helicopters and jets will be specifically tasked with searching them out and engaging them in air-to-air combat. The weapon mixes currently carried by many combat helicopters and jets would be utterly devastating were they to be used against rotary-winged aircraft. In the future, helicopters will therefore have to learn to fight a thrust-and-parry air battle of their own, just as the tank has had to learn to fend for itself in tank-to-tank duels. This air battle will be an almost entirely novel feature of warfare, since in most helicopter campaigns of the past – especially those in South Vietnam and Afghanistan – the side that had the helicopters was not opposed by enemy air power at all.

Counter-measures, more than armour, will save the helicopter

The helicopter's air battle will be quite different in scale and scope from the main deep-strike air battle of advanced fast jets with their airfield-cratering munitions and air-to-air missiles (AAMs). Nevertheless it will have the same general structure and will be fought according to similar basic rules. The humble helicopter will have to exploit its own special tactical agility to out-fight enemy attack helicopters and jets in the air: it will have to jink and dodge behind trees and other ground clutter, making split-second decisions whether or not to take the risk of pursuit across the FLOT, and it will have to dash, climb and manoeuvre at super-high speed, as only the latest attack helicopters can.

In addition to this, the helicopter will have to use its own brands of ECM, stealth technology and firepower to suppress the opposition. Devices to counter IR-homing warheads are already being fitted, in the form of exhaust-gas coolers and decoy strobes. However, there is still some way to go in areas such as radar jamming and suppression of the distinctive rotor-wash signature; the complete 'stealth helicopter' remains some way in the future.

Despite their shortcomings, helicopters, no less than jets, will have to clear a path through enemy air defences before they will be able to operate effectively. They will need to adopt the 'Wild Weasel' concept, and an EW helicopter will accompany any helicopter force and smooth its way to the target both by jamming and by direct air-to-ground strikes.

In general, all this implies that there will be a relative increase in the number of EW, SAM-busting and dog-fighting helicopters, compared to other types. There will also have to be new munitions and specialised EW pods developed to make this battle possible. The helicopter, in short, will have to start learning to take the air battle as seriously as it already takes the ground battle.

Rational analysis of the future battlefield and the helicopter's role on it ought to pay greater attention to the remarkable Harrier Vertical/Short Take Off & Landing (VSTOL) 'jump jet'. Like the helicopter, the Harrier does not need a formal airfield and can hover, while it can pack a much greater payload and can move at almost Mach 1. Because it is completely decoupled, relying on thrust rather than aerodynamic lift when it chooses, it can change direction in mid-air to confound incoming combat

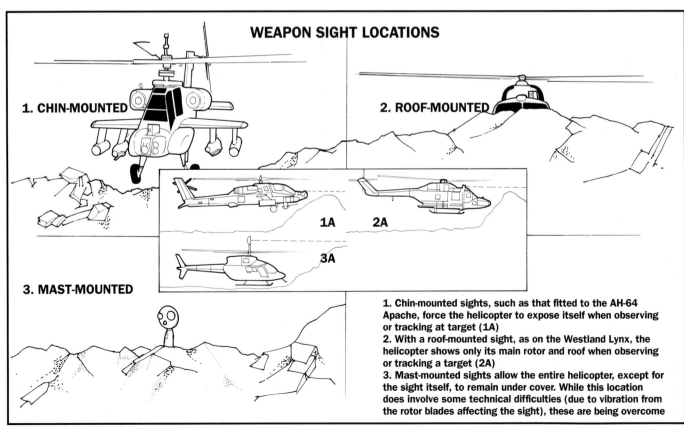

WEAPON SIGHT LOCATIONS

1. CHIN-MOUNTED

2. ROOF-MOUNTED

1A **2A**

3A

3. MAST-MOUNTED

1. Chin-mounted sights, such as that fitted to the AH-64 Apache, force the helicopter to expose itself when observing or tracking at target (1A)
2. With a roof-mounted sight, as on the Westland Lynx, the helicopter shows only its main rotor and roof when observing or tracking a target (2A)
3. Mast-mounted sights allow the entire helicopter, except for the sight itself, to remain under cover. While this location does involve some technical difficulties (due to vibration from the rotor blades affecting the sight), these are being overcome

ANTI-TANK HELICOPTER TACTICS

Tank-killing helicopters hunt in packs of perhaps half a dozen machines assisted by target-locating LOHs. Once the LOHs have identified a potentially fruitful enemy target, the team will first try to manoeuvre out of sight to a covered fire-position, perhaps behind a ridge or a treeline. From here, the LOHs – sitting 'rotor down' but still managing to keep the enemy in constant view through their mast-mounted scanners – may send tactical information to the fire team. This may be relayed by radio – if it is still working – or alternatively it may come in the form of target designation by laser.

With the enemy pinpointed, the attack helicopters will start to 'work' the target, each one bobbing into sight momentarily, firing and then quickly retreating into cover. Identified enemy air-defence weapons will be targeted first, then command tanks, and lastly ordinary tanks. If the ambush can be completed before the enemy takes cover or vectors effective counter-fire on to the helicopters, a team of six firing units could very

well expect to annihilate an entire battalion of 31 tanks in less than half an hour.

Even if it is forced to break off the engagement prematurely, or if it is fighting under-strength, the tank-hunting team can still hope to inflict serious losses on the enemy. Armoured formations will have to keep alert, not only so they can activate their own air defences, ECMs and other counter-measures, but also to call up artillery and anti-helicopter helicopters.

Helicopters currently rely on missiles and unguided rockets to attack hardened targets such as armoured vehicles – the GAU-8A cannon, as fitted to the A-10A Thunderbolt would probably stop a rotary-winged aircraft in its tracks. Should the helicopter come upon soft-skinned vehicles mixed in with the armour, however, then its guns will be brought into play. Both Soviet and NATO helicopters are armed for this eventuality, and future generations of attack helicopters are unlikely to lose their capacity to destroy vehicles and material so cheaply.

Above: The AH-1 Huey Cobra first saw service in Vietnam, where its small size and comparatively huge weapons load made it a firm favourite with hard-pressed ground troops. More recently, it has been recast in the anti-armour role, which it shares with its larger successor, the AH-64 Apache. Rocket-powered projectiles, whether guided or unguided, have the great advantage of not upsetting the weapons platform by their recoil, so are particularly well adapted to helicopter use

Fast troop-carrying helicopters, such as the UH-60 Blackhawk (Right), and the Mi-24 Hind (Below) have given the modern generation of infantryman a way of getting into battle quickly, and at minimum risk to himself in the dangerous moving-up period. The Soviet solution to the problem of how to protect the aircraft was to equip the helicopter as a gunship, so allowing it to put down massive suppressive fire before inserting a small group of infantrymen. The Blackhawk – a much bigger aircraft – relies on dedicated gunships to neutralise enemy forces

Left: The helicopter's short ferry range means that it, itself, must be airportable if it is to be of any use in the rapid-intervention role. One of the constraints placed on the designers of the UH-60 was that it should be transportable by the C-141 Starlifter, the frontline transport aircraft of the USAF's Military Airlift Command. They had to fold it a couple of times to achieve the desired result!

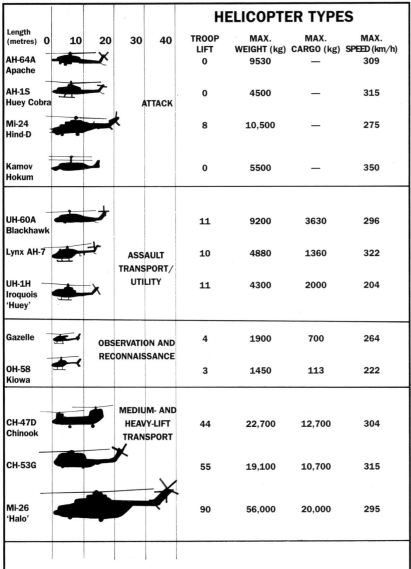

HELICOPTER TYPES

Length (metres) 0 10 20 30 40	TROOP LIFT	MAX. WEIGHT (kg)	MAX. CARGO (kg)	MAX. SPEED (km/h)
AH-64A Apache	0	9530	—	309
AH-1S Huey Cobra	0	4500	—	315
Mi-24 Hind-D	8	10,500	—	275
Kamov Hokum	0	5500	—	350
UH-60A Blackhawk	11	9200	3630	296
Lynx AH-7	10	4880	1360	322
UH-1H Iroquois 'Huey'	11	4300	2000	204
Gazelle	4	1900	700	264
OH-58 Kiowa	3	1450	113	222
CH-47D Chinook	44	22,700	12,700	304
CH-53G	55	19,100	10,700	315
Mi-26 'Halo'	90	56,000	20,000	295

Categories labelled in the chart: ATTACK; ASSAULT TRANSPORT/UTILITY; OBSERVATION AND RECONNAISSANCE; MEDIUM- AND HEAVY-LIFT TRANSPORT

aircraft and missiles alike; this gives it a crucial advantage in dog-fighting. In practice, 'viffing' (vectoring in flight) is not the sudden stop that some commentators would have one believe, but it is none the less effective for all that. Admittedly, when taking off and landing vertically, the Harrier has a very heavy IR signature, and it requires a larger support echelon than a helicopter and cannot transport troops. Nevertheless, in the microcosm of the overall air battle that is the helicopter battle, the Harrier is a lethal interloper.

Fixed- and rotary-wing aircraft compliment each other

More heavily 'hyped', although perhaps ultimately less promising than the Harrier, is the A-10A Thunderbolt II. This is a purpose-built tank-busting close-support fixed-wing jet, low, slow and heavily armoured. It mounts a heavy cannon as well as a wide variety of smart (and other) bombs. If it is allowed to manoeuvre close to the enemy, the A-10 is well able to take out AAA, SAMs, tanks and helicopters alike. However, its ability to survive is in some doubt, since it lacks the agility of an attack helicopter. And even if the A-10 does not fall victim to its intended target, it still needs to return to a large, fixed infrastructure, though not necessarily an airfield proper; A-10s on exercise have used straight stretches of autobahn as runways quite successfully, just the same as the Harrier.

It is certainly likely that a mixture of these fixed-wing aircraft will take part in the close-support air battle along with the helicopters. Relatively large numbers of unsophisticated light jets such as the Alpha Jet and the Hawk may be added to the brew as reinforcements for the Harriers and A-10s, making the sky over the FLOT more crowded than ever. This will surely intensify the nightmare of airspace management at the same time as it gives anti-aircraft

HELICOPTER WEAPONRY

Standard 7.62mm general-purpose machine guns (GPMGs) were originally fitted to transport helicopters, while on attack and LOH machines these were normally supplanted by electrically powered, hydraulically powered or blowback-powered multi-barrelled rotary aircraft guns. These weapons could fire between 1600 and 10,000 rounds per minute of ammunition ranging from standard 5.56mm and 7.62mm ball to 30mm HEAT and KE anti-tank rounds. The 40mm grenade- or bomblet-launcher has also traditionally been a mainstay of the helicopter's armoury; this can fire at a rate of up to 230 rounds per minute.

When the need for heavy firepower support for helicopter operations was originally recognised, the first thought was to transport underslung conventional artillery pieces to an advanced fire-position. This happened in the European powers' colonial wars, such as the Malayan Emergency (1948-60) and the Algerian Insurrection (1954-62), and 'displacing' artillery remains an important service that the helicopter can offer. However, in the 1960s, the Americans came up with another approach when they fitted massed 2.75in rocket pods on to the helicopters themselves.

This was the birth of aerial rocket artillery (ARA). At first up to 72 HE rockets, each weighing between 5 and 8kg, could be fired either individually or in salvoes to a range of up to 3km; today, the Soviets mount up to 128 2.24in rockets per helicopter. The great advantage of rockets is that they have no appreciable recoil to jar the helicopter, whereas the recoil from a number of guns can, at least initially, throw the aircraft violently out of alignment; the disadvantage is that rockets are not especially accurate.

From unguided rockets, the natural next step was to equip helicopters with guided weapons. Early on, the French pioneered heli-borne ATGW, and the move has captured the imagination of the world's armies. The classic US wire-guided TOW is today giving way to various 'fire and forget' systems that can follow the target once a laser beam has designated it or otherwise locked on to it. The AH-64 Apache can carry 16 Hellfire laser-guided AT missiles.

These anti-tank weapons have already been joined by guided weapons for other duties, such as dog-fighting or radiation-seeking; inevitably these will at some stage be joined by many more varieties. The attack helicopter of the future may well be capable, at least in theory, of firing a single salvo of four missiles that simultaneously downs an enemy helicopter, takes out an air-defence radar, kills a troop of tanks and makes a helicopter 'airfield' uninhabitable for 12 hours.

gunners yet more plentiful targets. Admittedly it also implies a bigger threat to the anti-aircraft gunners, but they will at least enjoy the defender's advantage of sitting in place waiting for targets, whereas the aircraft will have to seek them out actively and co-ordinate their efforts to destroy them.

The balance of advantage between attack and defence will vary widely according to local circumstances, but overall the defence is surely likely to have the upper hand. The aerial element of a future war may well resemble the standoff over the FLOT that marked the middle period of the 1973 October War. On that occasion both sides came to believe it was impossible to operate aircraft safely beyond the enemy's front line. It was only later in the war that the Israelis successfully carved out SAM-free corridors for air operations.

The attack helicopter's first task is to suppress local anti-aircraft fire

Quite apart from fighting its complex battle in the air, the helicopter will in future have to protect its own home base, just as the jets already do. The difference is that in the case of the helicopter, the 'airfield' may consist of little more than a forest clearing containing some POL trucks, a small ammunition train and a skeleton maintenance crew. Although helicopters can land in any field or small clearing – or even on a flat roof or at an urban crossroads – their overall mobility and operability is still quite severely limited by the mobility and vulnerability of their supporting rear echelon.

This soft-skinned echelon was previously highly secure, since it could be protected both by dispersal beyond the range of enemy artillery, and by making its signature so small and insignificant that it would be easily overlooked. In a future high-tech war, however, it is likely that neither of these arrangements will work. Even the smallest installation deep behind enemy lines may in future be perfectly visible at a considerable distance, while the greatly increased range of surface-to-surface gun and rocket weapons will make it entirely vulnerable once it has been located.

Insofar as helicopters depend on fuel, ammunition and maintenance, therefore, they are more at risk today than they ever were in the past. In Vietnam between 1965 and 1972 each machine needed at first three, then eventually 10 hours of maintenance for every hour in the air; in the future this ratio is unlikely to be significantly improved. Mechanical reliability is certainly on an upward curve, but so too is mechanical and electronic complexity, bringing with it increased potential for a systems failure somewhere down the line. As far as logistics are concerned, helicopter operation is by no means an easy option. In 1967 each brigade in the US 1st Cavalry Division (Airmobile) in Vietnam consumed some 250 tonnes of supplies per day. This is roughly equivalent to the 650 tonnes that an armoured division in Patton's Third Army needed to fight in Europe in 1944.

In Vietnam, helicopters needed 10 hours maintenance for one in the air

The general conclusion must be that, while the helicopter's 'home airfield' and logistic infrastructure are no less important to its survival today than they were in the 1960s, these essential lifelines have become very much more accessible targets for enemy attack. And the more dangerous the helicopter is thought to be to tanks and other ground units, the more ardently the enemy will seek new

While they are almost a generation apart, the AH-64 Apache (Far Left), and the Mi-24 Hind (Left) are inevitably compared one with the other. The Hind D, (not the most recent evolution, but the most common), mounts a four-barrel 12.7mm cannon in an electrically operated chin turret. Wing pylons accommodate four ATGWs – either AT-2 Swatters or AT-6 Spirals – and four UV-32-57 rocket pods. The Apache mounts a 30mm M230A1 chain gun and up to 16 Hellfire anti-tank missiles, but an air-to-air version, fitted with Sparrows and Sidewinders, is on the stocks

The British and American armies both use 155mm towed howitzers, as well as the self-propelled version. Both the British FH-70 (Left) and the US M198 (Above) are capable of firing the Copperhead cannon-launched guided projectile (Above left), as are the M109A2 and Abbot SPGs. Copperhead is said to be so accurate that it can be dropped down the open hatch of a moving tank from up to 16km away

is much the same in all modern armies. The battery is controlled by the battery command post, which consists of signallers, computer operators and command post officers. They employ three radio nets: the battery net connects the battery with the battery commander and his forward observers; the regimental net connects the batteries, forward observers and battery commanders with the commanding officer; and the regimental logistic net controls the delivery of ammunition to the batteries, according to battle requirements.

A battery may operate as a single entity, or it may split into two troops, each with its own command post, capable of operating independently of each other. Because artillery is constantly in action, there is always an alternative command post in existence. Even when the battery is operating as one unit, the two command posts will take turns to control it. For example, the alternative post would take over while the main command is

PRINCIPLES OF ARTILLERY FIRE PLANNING

Surprise and shock action are the artillery's stock-in-trade. Most casualties occur in the target area in the first seconds of a firing mission, as incoming shells catch troops diving for the cover of trenches and pulling down the hatches of armoured vehicles. After the initial shock action, artillery can only really keep the enemy's heads down, unless heavier calibres are being used or lucky shells hit armoured vehicles or enter trenches.

Initially, therefore, as much artillery ammunition as possible must be put on to the target in as short a time as possible, preferably with the first salvo striking home. The process of adjustment, although guaranteeing that fire on a target will soon be accurate, gives a warning, and surprise and shock action are often lost. It is also preferable to co-ordinate several batteries to fire in a burst on to one target as this is dramatically more effective as a shock weapon (and the chances of direct hits are higher) than just using one battery – even though the same number of rounds might be fired overall.

Ammunition must be carefully tailored to the target. Proximity ammunition that explodes overhead is particularly useful if fired without warning at troops in the open or at armoured vehicles travelling with hatches up. Judicious mixtures of ammunition are often used. For example, HE mixed with Delay is useful once troops have gone to ground in trenches (and some Smoke and Proximity may increase the confusion), while mixing HE with Smoke deters anyone from trying to extinguish the burning smoke canisters, though HE must always be ready to be fired as an alternative if a smoke screen proves not to be effective. It is important that rounds land at exactly the times ordered (to the second); for this reason everyone involved in an operation must synchronise his watch with that of the artillery commander.

Time must be allowed for the batteries to switch targets – one minute for light calibres, and more for heavier calibres. To maintain fire on a target when several batteries are operating, target switches can be staggered. Batteries must be kept 'superimposed', so that guns may switch to opportunity targets without affecting the fire plan.

When the artillery is covering a friendly infantry or armoured advance, fire on the objective should always be adjusted. This can be done either before the advance begins or even while it is taking place. As attacking troops enter the near edge of the fall of shot, the FO creeps it forward on to the enemy's rear positions.

in transit to a new location and when it is necessary to rest key personnel.

The guns themselves also need rest. At any one time, one gun is likely to be out of action for routine servicing – barrel bores must be kept clean, recoil systems topped up with hydraulic fluid and barrels changed from time to time. There will also be mechanical breakdowns and battle damage to contend with. The gun batteries themselves remain back on the gun line, out of reach of enemy direct-fire weapons, and rely for guidance on information passed back by forward observers. The FO's job is to control scheduled fire and find targets of opportunity. Organised in teams of three, and assigned to infantry companies and armoured squadrons, FOs work alongside the company (or armoured squadron) commander, maintaining radios on the company and battalion nets; they follow the battle closely, bringing down fire on targets that they detect for themselves, or on request.

Artillery has changed in its own basic technology

In the attack, the FO moves with the 'point' platoon. As the leading platoons approach enemy positions, he directs the artillery fire forward, keeping the worst of it just in front of the leading troops. Although the attackers may suffer some casualties from their own artillery, the enemy will not be able to engage them from their trenches until the very last moment.

During the attack, one FO will usually set up an 'anchor' OP, from which he can observe the operation in relative safety. With good radio communications between himself, the attacking force, other

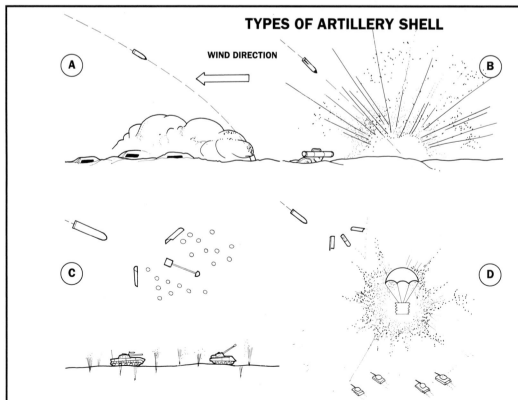

TYPES OF ARTILLERY SHELL

WIND DIRECTION

(A)

(B)

(C)

(D)

Apart from guided projectiles such as Copperhead, the artillery has a variety of ammunition types to draw on for different tasks:

A. SMOKE
Used to conceal movement

B. HIGH EXPLOSIVE (HE)
Used against point or area targets. Also available in this category are White Phosphorous (WP) shells.

C. 'CARGO' (Scatterable sub-munitions).
Include both anti-armour and anti-personnel mines. Also used to deliver objects such as disposable jammers

D. ILLUMINATION
Flares suspended below small parachutes (duration: about 30 seconds)

FOs and the guns, the observer in the anchor OP can co-ordinate fire: particularly important when assaulting observers lose radio communications or are killed or wounded.

The introduction of a new generation of armoured command and control vehicles, such as the USA's Emerson FIre Support Team Vehicle (FISTV) and the British Army's Warrior Observation Party Vehicle (OPV) will enlarge the FO's responsibilities considerably. Thus mounted, FOs will be able to keep up with the advancing armour, and stay at the forefront of the battle. However, there is one drawback. These vehicles are manifestly not tanks, so when working with armoured units, FOs, who are already among the highest priority targets on the modern battlefield, are likely to attract even more attention than they do at present.

As well as providing this new mobility for its eyes and ears, the artillery has changed in its own basic technology, too. The destructive power of

TYPES OF ARTILLERY FUZE

Artillery shells perform different functions according to how they are fuzed:

A. PROXIMITY AIRBURST
Contains a miniature radar, which emits a beam during flight, and detonates the shell at the correct distance

B. 'MECHANICAL TIME' AIRBURST
Contains a timer (1), which is set before the shell is fired

C. 'POINT DETONATING, QUICK TIME'
Detonates the shell as soon as it hits a solid object

D. DELAYED ACTION
A column of slow-burning explosive ignites on initial impact (1). When this has burnt through, it ignites the main charge (2)

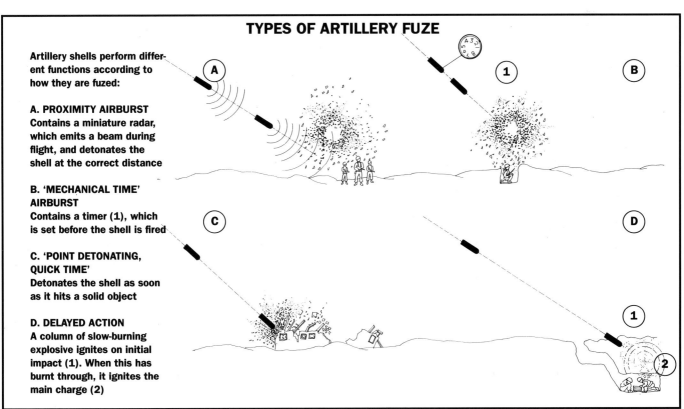

even the simple HE shell has increased dramatically in the last decade, though limits on the size and weight of shell that can be fired probably preclude further development. Instead, artillery ammunition is becoming more 'mission-oriented', using sophisticated warheads to hit point targets. Thus the explosive punch is directed much more accurately to where it will do the most damage.

Among these new weapons are Precision Guided Munitions (PGMs), such as the USA's Copperhead round. Fired from a 155mm gun, the Copperhead projectile homes on to a target illuminated by a laser designator aimed by the FO. An individual tank is thus vulnerable to individual artillery shells.

Artillery ammunition is becoming more 'mission orientated'

Terminally-Guided Sub-Munitions (TGSMs) are also intended to kill individual tanks, but without human intervention. TGSM shells burst over the general target area, releasing sub-munitions that float to earth under small parachutes. Relying on their own sensors to locate moving targets, they attack the vulnerable top armour of tanks, using shaped charges to achieve penetration. The MLRS's TGSM, with six sub-missiles that seek, track and home in on tanks, should be in service by the end of the century. With the right sort of fuzing for top-cover attack it will be a serious 'assault breaker' and force multiplier.

Both PGMs and TGSMs can destroy specific targets in the same manner as direct-fire weapons, but without the restrictions imposed by line-of-sight target acquisition. Furthermore, the accuracy of these sub-munitions will not depend on the operator's vision (which is often impaired by dust, mist

or smoke on the battlefield), nor by the weather or the condition of the gun, all of which greatly restrict the effectiveness of direct-fire weapons.

These new projectiles can be controlled from inside a vehicle by just one man, who has no need to expose himself to the enemy in order to acquire his target and destroy it. Tied into a comprehensive system of battlefield surveillance and communications, he can orchestrate a colossal instantaneous barrage in total isolation from the actual weapon delivery systems themselves, so that his position will not be compromised by the guns' own IR and sound signature and still guarantee a significant number of one-hit kills.

Today, greater range allows guns to engage the enemy earlier

Supporting the contact battle is only part of the modern artillery's role. In the fluid fighting of World War II's European theatre, artillery was mainly used in the close support role. Today, greater range allows guns to engage the enemy earlier, in the depth-fire battle, breaking up enemy columns long before they fire a shot, hammering resupply routes and shattering enemy morale before the fight has even been joined.

Its extra range and increased accuracy means that the priorities for the use of artillery will have to be rethought. The cosy concept of every infantry or armour commander having his own artillery unit on call will disappear. On the battlefield of the future, competition for artillery assets will be fierce, the demands of the depth-fire battle often overriding the needs of the contact battle. The manoeuvre arms will at last become occupiers of ground won by artillery, but armour and infantry will hold this ground only if the artillery

Above: The mapboard is still essential to the Forward Observation (FO) Officer when he is planning fire missions

Left: The control and monitoring panel for a Heron-26 RPV battery. The drone aircraft is controlled from here, and the pictures it sends back inspected and recorded

TYPES OF ARTILLERY AMMUNITION

High Explosive shells can have either 'point detonating' fuzes, which explode on impact, or 'delay' fuzes, which allow the round to penetrate before exploding, collapsing trenches or exploding inside buildings. HE can also be fitted with 'Variable Time' (VT) fuzes – either the old-fashioned 'mechanical time' or the more accurate, faster 'proximity' fuzes – which explode the shell at a set height above the ground, showering the splinters forwards and downwards in a shotgun effect. Against troops in the open, particularly if fired without any warning, VT fuzes are lethal.

Against unprotected people, particularly in the jungle, 'flechette' rounds are used. These shells contain thousands of darts – flechettes – which are often made of plastic so as not to show up on hospital X Rays. In Vietnam, Viet Cong victims of flechettes were often discovered completely impaled against trees.

Another nasty anti-personnel weapon is the exploding shell packed with White Phosphorus (WP). On contact with the air, phosphorus ignites, producing intense heat and thick, white smoke. Phosphorus will burn through clothes and flesh, the water of the human body further encouraging the chemical reaction. The burning, which is excruciatingly painful, can only be stopped by cutting away all flesh containing phosphorus.

Smoke is delivered using a shell with a base that ejects the contents when over the target. The smoke takes a minute to build up, each canister burning for several minutes, producing thick, white smoke. Smoke rounds are used to conceal forces from the enemy, during an advance or a withdrawal, for example. They are quite the opposite to 'marker' rounds, which produce a coloured smoke to indicate targets to attacking aircraft or to signal one's own position – for example, in dense jungle.

depth-fire battle is successful in preventing enemy reinforcements from counter-attacking.

Although all guns within range can be used for depth-fire targets, it is usually the heavy guns at corps level and above that are entrusted with the task. Those guns are often deployed as close to the Front Line of Own Troops (FLOT) as the close support artillery, so their extra range can be used to reach as far as possible into the enemy's rear areas.

The greatest threat to artillery is fire from enemy artillery batteries

Because the depth-fire battle is fought beyond the limits of the FOs' vision, it depends on a wide variety of other means of target acquisition. At the higher formation headquarters, the artillery cell will co-ordinate the various means of target acquisition at its disposal, such as sound ranging and mortar and gun locating radars, special forces teams acting as observation parties, and monitoring the enemy's radio transmissions to locate his headquarters and artillery positions.

One further advance in depth-fire target acquisition is the drone or Remotely-Piloted Vehicle (RPV). Until now, the forward observer was the artillery's only means of 'real-time' target observation and aquisition, but today RPVs such as Phoenix and Cobra send back pictures as they fly, enabling

missions to be fired immediately. Drone flights over enemy rear areas identify his artillery batteries, headquarters and logistic areas, as well as resupply routes. The depth-fire battle will extend as far as RPVs will allow the guns and rockets to reach, making all rear areas liable to accurate artillery attack.

Although the depth-fire battle must start as early as possible in order to prevent the enemy reaching the contact battle, the timing and weight of this fire must be incorporated into the overall battle plan. The heavy guns are particularly vulnerable to counter-battery fire so must be used judiciously. While guns sit mute, they are safe, but completely useless; once they have been fired they must be moved. Decisions to 'unmask' the heavies are taken at a high level.

The Counter-Battery (CB) battle – that is, knocking out enemy artillery – is fought at divisional level and higher, using 175mm and larger calibre guns and rockets. The greatest threat to artillery is fire from enemy artillery batteries, and modern technology is reducing the time it takes to detect the gun positions and then fire back. The only certain way of avoiding counter-battery fire is for guns to fire in bursts, then move at least 500m, so that the incoming fire lands on an empty position. However, it is unacceptable to have artillery break off in the middle of a fire plan, or not available while ensuring its own safety by moving.

ARTILLERY RANGE AND ACCURACY

The range of an artillery piece is governed by the strength of its propellant charge – and that is limited by the physical strength of the gun barrel. The most successful attempts to increase the range of a big gun have concentrated on rocket-assisted projectiles (HERA – High Explosive Rocket Assist), which supplement the power of the original charge with a small motor in the base of the shell, or by setting off secondary charges in sub-chambers, part-way up the barrel. At such extreme ranges, accuracy is impossible to sustain, since even a small error in laying the gun, or a small inaccuracy in either barrel or projectile, will send the shell literally miles off target. Thus, only objects the size of towns are worth targeting. Small inaccuracies in elevation are more costly than errors in direction, due to the magnifying effect of the shell's parabolic trajectory

100 PER CENT ZONE
The zone gets longer at greater distances

Range has increased progressively over the last 100 years:

GUN TYPE:	RANGE (km):
1. WWI 8in Gun	15
2. 105mm	22
3. 155mm	30
4. 175mm HERA	37
5. Krupps 80cm K(E)	47
6. MLRS Phase 3	60
7. Paris Gun	70
8. HARP cannon	185
9. Iraqi 'Supergun'	??

FIELD ARTILLERY ACCURACY

The artillery concept of accuracy is often misunderstood by soldiers used to direct-fire weapons. Whereas direct-fire weapons either hit or miss specific targets, artillery is an area weapon. Even if set into a concrete mounting, an individual gun would not place 100 shells into the same shell-hole. This is because the inherent characteristics of a gun barrel cause every round to behave very slightly differently during firing. The shells actually land in a large cigar-shaped pattern called the '100 per cent zone'. In the same way a machine gun on a rock-solid mounting will spray bullets into a 'beaten zone', and even the most accurate precision small arms will 'group' its shots.

When a battery fires, the rounds land in the same pattern as the layout of the gun position, with each gun covering its own 100 per cent zone. This reproduction of the gun position layout occurs because the guns are carefully aligned when a battery moves into its location. First 'battery centre' (that is, the centre of the battery position) is accurately established and then an operation known as 'passing of line' takes place, whereby each gun is lined up to fire in exactly the same direction. The accuracy of artillery fire then depends upon the FOs sending the guns precise target information.

However, when several batteries are firing on the same target, optimum accuracy happens only when each battery is surveyed into a common grid, or survey grid – each to the same level of accuracy. This process is similar in principle to the 'passing of line' from director to guns on battery positions, but is carried out by the 'locators', using the latest surveying instruments to bring the common 'line', or bearing, to each battery. When several batteries fire at the same target, they use the FO's grid reference as the centre of the target, and the rounds fall within around 200m of this reference.

From the diagram of the 100 per cent zone, it is obvious that shells coming from behind and flying overhead are more liable to fall short and explode among friendly troops. Similarly, shells fired from a flank appear to spread over a large area lateral to the front line – even though they will in fact be on target. It is the job of the FOs to advise unit commanders when close-in fire is likely to be dangerous, so commanders can decide whether to risk injuries to their own men.

The different characteristics of special types of ammunition must also be borne in mind. Illuminating shells, for instance, can be blown in the wrong direction by wind changes, making them a real double-edged weapon. Wind changes and temperature similarly affect smoke, delivered in base-ejection shells. Hot, rising air can make smoke pillar, diminishing or even eliminating its screening effect. Smoke shells must also land well in front of enemy positions, as water will easily extinguish the canisters.

Above: A Forward Observation Officer. Artillery almost always fires at greater ranges than the gunners themselves can see, so an experienced officer has to be positioned far enough forward to be able to gauge where the artillery shells are falling, and order changes of direction and elevation accordingly

Left: The gunner's view of an M198 155mm howitzer

Below: Computer technology allows a number of fire missions to be pre-planned down to the finest detail, and then called up with just a few key strokes. Battlefield computers need to be hardened against EMP – the pulse of radiation created by a nuclear explosion, probably high in the atmosphere

Current doctrine has it that if batteries move every couple of hours they remain one step ahead of incoming counter-battery fire. With artillery expected to begin firing early in the war – and remain in action throughout – the constant 'shooting and scooting' will be exhausting and severely debilitating. A likely scenario has batteries moving not to completely new locations, but around a circuit or within an overall gun area. Battery positions may also be split into two smaller troop areas, and the whole spread over more ground than usual, so that at least part of a battery might be unaffected by accurate CB fire. A fully prepared alternative position nearby is sensible, too, allowing individual guns to be moved quickly out of danger, with the minimum of disruption to their own activities.

All these solutions to the CB problem require large areas of land to be allocated to the artillery. Apart from the premium on actual grid squares for alternate gun positions, no-one is going to be too happy at having a gun battery next door that draws enemy artillery fire, then pushes off before it arrives!

Winning the counter-battery battle depends completely on accurate target designation. While general artillery targets at this level are identified for the depth battle by RPVs, special forces teams, and SIGINT, the CB battle is fought using data mainly from locating units. Locating artillery encompasses a wide range of different skills and tasks. Sound ranging uses strings of microphones to triangulate bearings to enemy gun positions in relation to the sound of their firing. Radar location equipment calculates enemy battery locations by detecting shells in their irregular parabolic trajectories, and RPVs fly over enemy territory and photograph depth targets.

The regular collection of meteorological data is also vital to the accuracy of field gunnery. Helium-filled balloons acting as remote radar stations double as weather stations, sending back air temperatures and densities, wind speed and direction, at vertical intervals of 15m. Every few hours, battery command post computers are up-dated with new 'met', greatly increasing the accuracy of the firing data they calculate for the guns.

Every few hours, battery command post computers are updated

Despite all this, the gunners are not constrained by sophistications. If they have to, forward observers can still make their own maps simply by firing the guns on given bearings and elevations, then plotting the fall of shot on to blank graph paper. Then they can adjust the fire taking these bearings as their reference points, whether the round has landed anywhere near the target or not.

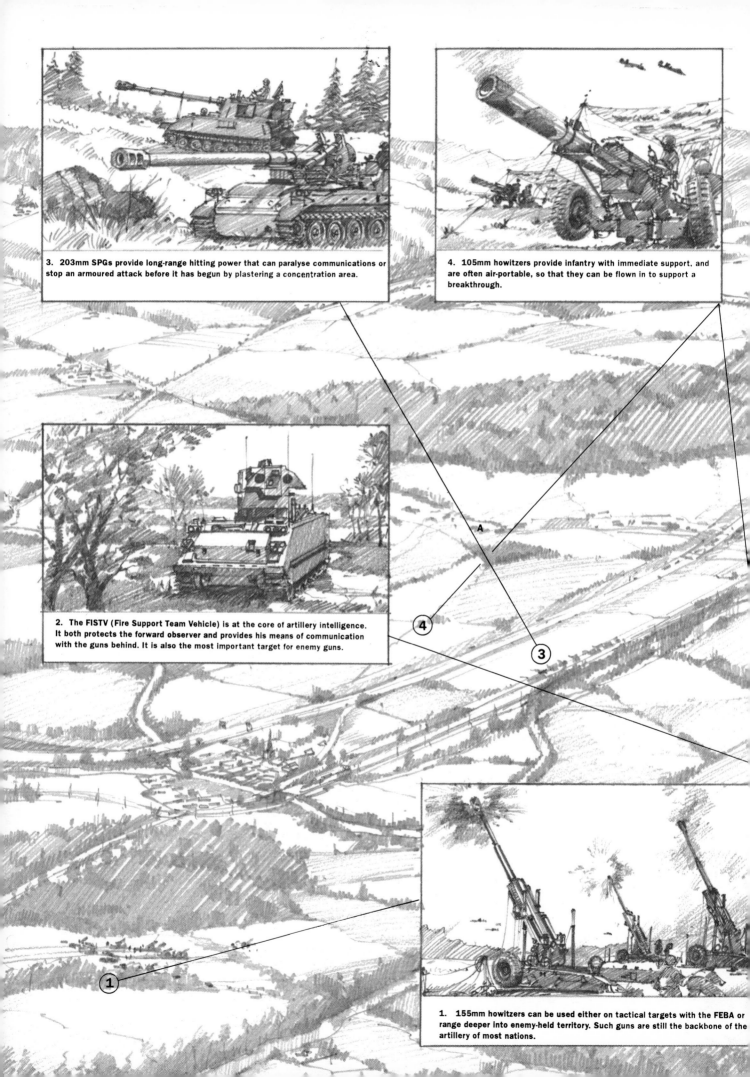

3. 203mm SPGs provide long-range hitting power that can paralyse communications or stop an armoured attack before it has begun by plastering a concentration area.

4. 105mm howitzers provide infantry with immediate support, and are often air-portable, so that they can be flown in to support a breakthrough.

2. The FISTV (Fire Support Team Vehicle) is at the core of artillery intelligence. It both protects the forward observer and provides his means of communication with the guns behind. It is also the most important target for enemy guns.

1. 155mm howitzers can be used either on tactical targets with the FEBA or range deeper into enemy-held territory. Such guns are still the backbone of the artillery of most nations.

5. As their electronics have improved, so RPVs have become more and more important in getting information from behind enemy lines - even when fired on successfully by AAA, they reveal the position of such guns which then become vulnerable.

6. Despite new and improved armour, tanks and AFV's are still vulreable to modern artillery-launched sub-munitions. They're obvious, too - so they would be a priority target.

7. MLRS are one of the most feared modern weapons systems, because of the weight of fire and the range of munitions they can put down within a short space of time.

THE ARTILLERY
KING OF THE BATTLEFIELD?

A typical arrangement of modern artillery, with the front line (A) running at 90 degrees across a major communications route. At the FEBA (Forward Edge of Battle Area) itself, the most noticeable artillery presence would be small pieces, such as the air-portable 105mm howitzer, giving immediate direct support to an infantry battalion. The most important artillery presence at FEBA, however, are the observers, in armoured vehicles or well dug in. They can call down an immense weight of fire from the batteries behind them, and on any battlefield are the most marked men. Behind the front line, the artillery is deployed in two main parks, and consists of 203mm SPGs and 105mm conventional artillery pieces. The 105s guns can be directed either onto targets within the FEBA or at deeper targets, while the 203s will normally be used exclusively on these deeper targets - supply lines, enemy batteries, armoured concentrations or headquarters. Information on where the enemy can be hit hard may come from piloted reconnaissance aircraft or even from satellites; it is, however, very likely to come from RPVs (Remotely Piloted Vehicles) - drones that can be catapulted up at any time and are expendable.
The final element in the equation are the MLRS (Multiple Launch Rocket Systems) that can put down the biggest weight of fire. They can be used for any task that requires a swift response - crushing down on a tank attack, scattering an air-launched minefield, or putting in fuel-air explosions over enemy infantry dug-in in a town. They are on the road and have to be ready to move very quickly, as they are prime targets for counter-battery fire.

Below: The Germans built their biggest guns in fortifications. This one, on the Somme, had to be abandoned when the British offensive got under way

Artillery is limited in its maximum range and in the payload it can deliver. The USSR adopted the Self-Propelled (SP) system in the 1970s, and underlined its overall artillery superiority with the range advantage these weapons had, over equivalent NATO systems. The West tried to counter this superiority by extending the range of its existing guns, and the development of Extended Range Full Bore (ERFB) base-bleed ammunition was one attempt to redress the balance. The principle of ERFB is to fit a light projectile that is smaller than the bore of the gun barrel into a jacket that does fit the bore. The rifling in the barrel acts on this to give the round spin, and it is discarded when it leaves the barrel.

TARGET: PARIS

The advances over the course of the last 100 years in both the accuracy and the range of artillery fire have more than kept pace with requirements. When Krupps unveiled its rifled artillery piece at the Paris Exhibition of 1868, it attracted little attention. Just two years later, the people of Paris were to find out the hard way just how effective this gun could be when the Prussians besieged their city and bombarded them from a range (A) much greater than their own antiquated pieces could reach (B). And in WWI, it was Paris that was again the target for yet another revolutionary development – the Paris Gun, as it became known. This time, the battery was sited more than 60km away (C)

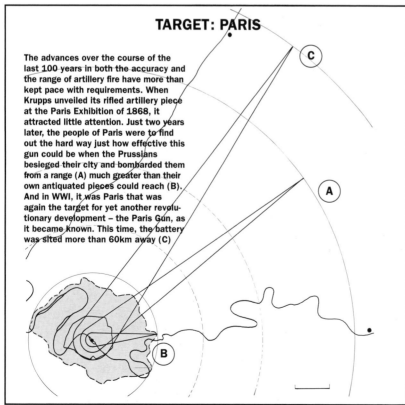

When Maxim first produced an effective automatic weapon, he changed the face of the battlefield overnight. Today, the medium and heavy machine gun (Left), of either 5.56mm, 7.62mm or 12.7mm calibre still dominates at short ranges of up to a mile

advanced communication consoles – while responsibility for the prosecution of the actual fighting rests with lance corporals commanding fireteams or half-sections. With increased weapon power and widely dispersed by the speed of the battle, a tactical unit of just four or eight men may well be the largest that can operate independently.

This development promises radical changes in the military pecking order, raising the status of the infantry. In future only the very ablest men will be capable of fulfilling the duties required of a junior infantry commander. As early as the Normandy battles of July 1944, the Allies were giving far too low a priority to the quality of their infantry. As a result, it was either consumed or its cutting edge badly blunted long before it could attain its objectives.

The infantryman must be trained and equipped to fight and win

The problem is still with us today, since the attractive high-tech arms – the air force, armour, engineering and artillery – still tend to take precedence in personnel selection. Thus the infantry may find that it is unable to achieve in practice many of the things that might be technically or theoretically within its grasp, due simply to skill deficiencies.

Elite infantry units will escape this fate because of the high standard of their selection process, but in many armies the line infantry will be unable to cope with the sudden enlargement of its responsibilities. Only a revolution in the way infantry is viewed and thus in the perception of the quality of manpower it requires will avert this possibility.

Yet even the ablest infantrymen will find the modern battlefield a severe test, not least due to communications problems, and the resulting call for him to use his own initiative under extreme

Because it is easier to drop grenades than throw them upwards, and easier to run downstairs than up, the preferred method of clearing buildings is from top to bottom.

Flame is a potent weapon in FIBUA. It is much easier to burn the enemy out of a house than to clear it room by room. The short maximum range of flame throwers is not a limitation, because of the confined nature of the battle.

Some armies believe in bringing artillery into built-up areas in the direct fire role, even using multi-barrel rocket launchers over open sights. Such weapons can be devastating, but they are often vulnerable to small arms and mortar fire.

Ta
blo
de

FIGHTING IN BUILT-UP AREAS

FIBUA is very much an infantry battle. While the other arms play vital supporting roles it is a soldier with rifle and grenades who must fight from building to building and room to room. Fields of fire are usually short, except down streets, and observation difficult. Smoke and dust limit visibility, while rubble inhibits vehicles. The abundance of cover and the distortion of sound by the buildings make locating snipers very difficult, while the comparative openness of the streets requires movement to be within buildings or underground. FIBUA is a three-dimensional battle, with troops fighting up and down buildings and attackers "outflanking" defenders by going through cellars and attics. Sometimes, one side may control the cellars and sewers of a street while the other controls everything above ground level. This type of fighting demands the highest levels of fitness, aggression and determination among the troops, and the highest standard of leadership from junior commanders.

Command and control during FIBUA is particularly difficult. Platoon and section commanders cannot see their men because they are in different rooms and different buildings. Buildings frequently block radio signals.

In FIBUA, the fighting is at very close quarters, with the two sides often in adjacent rooms. One man in a corridor can hold up an entire company, because a building is so confined. At such short ranges, the grenade is the key weapon.

ortant part to play in FIBUA - destroying strong points and alls ("mouseholes") for the infantry to enter buildings. The off-route mines and anti-armour weapons to defeat them.

Subterranean passageways, such as sewers, holes between cellars and underground railways, have a vital part to play in FIBUA. They can be casualty evacuation and ammunition resupply routes, or an attacker may use them to get underneath a defender and surprise him.

Below: Lightweight ATGWs such as the MILAN give the individual the power to kill even MBTs over short ranges. The term 'lightweight', however, is strictly relative – these weapons still represent a very heavy individual load for a man on foot, especially one under the stress of battle conditions, and perhaps encumbered by protective clothing to fend off NBC attack

pressure. Dismounted from its vehicles, today's infantry lacks effective personal intercommunication. There are plans to equip infantrymen with personal radios, but for now they are limited to shouted orders and hand signals that cannot convey all the necessary information and instructions. In defensive positions, where the infantry attempts to hide itself in widely dispersed camouflaged positions that separate each man from his comrades, communication of any sort becomes actually impossible. Besides being physically out of touch with their commander, the men feel psychologically isolated.

The infantryman's will to fight and win is still the most important factor

Then there is the challenge of continuous battle. Sensitive electronic equipment will have to be monitored throughout a 24-hour battle, and an exhausted operations officer who dozes over his IR or radar display may miss far more than the traditional sentry dozing behind the front-line wire. Conditions will be even more testing if the battle must be fought closed down in NBC suits.

In some futuristic projections, such as the 1985 US AirLand Battle 2000 (since revised as Army 21), the infantryman is aided in his fight against combat stress by pre-recorded video messages from his unit chaplain, and against boredom by playing computer games. His mail is digitised to be read straight off the computer screen. He is protected from the sight of mutilated bodies by disintegrating foam, and from fatigue, shock and his own inconvenient bodily functions by 'safe' drugs. In some scenarios he even has a personal jet-pack or heli-pack for flying short distances. (Such packs do exist, but it is surely beyond belief that they will ever be used for anything other than very specialised applications.)

On a more basic level, the front-line soldier will at least enjoy better armour protection than any of his predecessors since the Renaissance. Not only will he have the protection of his IFV, but also personal upper body armour and mine-resistant boots to complement the protective helmet – now made from plastic rather than the traditional steel – and these will go some way towards shielding him from low-velocity rounds and shell, mine or grenade fragments.

New generations of combat dress will contain multi-sensor camouflage features – to reduce the soldier's IR signature, for example – and, looking further into the future, he may have a miniaturised communications console and surveillance sight built into his helmet. His first-aid kit will be more sophisticated than in the past, too. For example, the Falklands conflict of 1982 taught the British the value of saline drips for battlefield first aid. The infantryman will thus be better equipped to treat wounded comrades, but to do so effectively he will need more extensive training.

A lone infantryman today outguns a World War II section

Infantry armament is also in transition. The future rifleman's personal weapon is likely to fire 'hypervelocity' caseless sabot rounds as do the still-experimental US 5.56/4.32mm Advanced Combat Rifle and the German H&K G11, and carry optical sights like the SUSAT fitted to the British 5.56mm SA80; it might even mount thermal or radar imagers. Automatically-loaded grenade-launchers, more powerful than the combat-proven US 40mm M79s and M16-mounted M203s of the 1960s are in the process of introduction. Already the Red Army has its AGS-17, and the US Marine Corps fields the Mk19. Hand grenades themselves have greater powers of fragmentation than ever, not to mention their diversification into

INFANTRY FIGHTING VEHICLES & APCs

In the past, the Infantry Fighting Vehicle has been little more than an armoured and lightly armed truck, but since the early 1980s, the state of the art has changed considerably. The future IFV may in many ways be a more complex vehicle than the tank itself. While it doesn't have a powerful main gun, it does mount an effective cannon and is set to take on much of the tank's advanced armour and EW hardware. On top of this, the IFV is the 'mothership' for an infantry squad which will fight either from it, or – more difficult to monitor and control from the vehicle – dismounted. A new generation of personal communications hardware – in development now for many years – looks set to change that, but of course it won't really make the transition from dismounted any easier. The current generation, which must be regarded as technologically transitional or intermediate, includes the following vehicles:-

Name:	1 Marder	2 BMP	3 AMX 10P	4 YW531	5 Bradley	6 Warrior
Origin:	W. Germany	USSR	France	China	USA	UK
Speed:(km/h)	78	56	65	65	78	75
Range (km):	500	440	500	500	500	600
Weight (tons):	28	13	14	12.6	23	25.3
Crew	10	11	11	14	9	10

ARMAMENT:
1: 1 x 20mm, 1 x 7.62mm MG
2: 1 x 73m,m gun or or 1 x 30mm cannon
  1 x Sagger AT or Spandrel missile, 1 x 7.62mm MG
3: 1 x 20mm, 1 x 7.62mm MG
4: 1 x 12.7mm MG
5: Twin TOW AT missiles, 1 x 25mm chain gun, 1 x 7.62mm MG
6: 1 x 30mm, 1 x 7.62mm MG

The sappers (military engineers) gained their name from their original task: 'sapping', or undermining and blowing up, fortifications on behalf of besieging armies. Now their job in the attack is to open the route, improve roads, breach enemy minefields, destroy obstacles and build bridges. In defence, too, it is the engineers who will choose and prepare the position, constructing (or at least, directing the building of) its fortifications, laying out its mines and obstacles, wrecking its approach roads and demolishing key bridges.

Below: Bridging operations are the task most frequently undertaken by combat engineers. These men of the United States Army are maneuvering pontoon sections into place to negotiate a major obstacle

Air forces, too, need engineers – to repair cratered runways and to build refuelling facilities at forward airstrips, as they did for British Harrier jets in the 1982 Falklands campaign. With hindsight, we can see that had the Argentines used their engineers as effectively, their air force could have based its attack aircraft at Stanley, so increasing their loiter time by a factor of four, with potentially devastating results.

The engineers' business is to change the very landscape of the battlefield if necessary, to channel the direction and shape of combat. Their role is so important that parts of it often spill over into other arms that are not specialised as engineers. For example, mine rollers and scissors bridges are carried by tanks that sappers man but which travel with armoured columns. Artillery or helicopter forces can scatter mines, and crossroads – and even major highways – are kept open by military police. For the sake of convenience in the present chapter all engineer-related tasks will be considered together, and treated as part of an overall 'engineer' approach to the battlefield.

Above: Most bridges will have been destroyed by enemy forces as they fall back. Here, sappers have installed charges which will be detonated remotely as and when the position becomes untenable

Left: While much bridge building is now performed at least semi-automatically, there is still a great deal of hard physical labour to be done

Another problem of definition is that in some – generally conscript – armies the duties of the engineers have been deliberately fragmented. Certain armies make the distinction between 'offensive' (or 'mobility') engineering and 'defensive' (or 'counter-mobility') engineering. Other armies divide their engineers on a rather different basis – into front-line 'combat pioneers' and rear-echelon 'construction troops'.

These arrangements aim to ensure that each type of engineer will immediately have available the specialised skills and equipment he needs for the particular task in hand, and will be able to deploy them very rapidly. They have the corresponding disadvantage of inflexibility. When circumstances demand that task-trained engineers cross over into other areas of specialisation, they often find it hard to adapt themselves to unfamiliar jobs, and may not have the right equipment readily to hand.

Generally, however, the majority of engineers are ready to turn their hand to anything. This versatility allows them to switch back and forth between offensive and defensive tasks, or between pioneering and construction, according to the dynamics of the battle. They keep a big 'golf bag' of skills and equipment from which they can select the most appropriate 'club' for the task at hand. The problem is that responsiveness may be impaired, and time lost, while a particular 'club' – which means equip-

RESERVE BRIDGE DEMOLITIONS

The first rule of reserve bridge demolition is to clear and then garrison the surrounding area, making sure that all ground, air and water-borne approaches to the objective are carefully watched. The garrison's task is to prevent the enemy seizing the bridge by *coup de main* before it can be demolished. The German offensive into Holland in 1940, for example, included a flying-boat seizure of a key bridge in central Rotterdam, and the US offensive to the Rhine in March 1945 included an armoured infantry seizure of the rail bridge at Remagen. Securing a bridge effectively *always* requires an all-arms effort, and that means protecting against attacks from aircraft, helicopters, armour, infantry and frogmen.

The next task is to wire up the bridge itself for demolition. Timing is of the essence. The bridge must not be blown too soon, because friendly troops may be stranded on the far side or imminent operations across it may be prevented; and it must not be blown too late, because the enemy may arrive in force to seize it. To make sure nothing can interfere, the engineer responsible for blowing the bridge must remain in close contact with the senior officer responsible for running the general battle.

When the time comes, all friendly troops – including the bridge garrisons – must first be withdrawn from the far bank. This may well prove difficult, since they may be in contact with the enemy, and find it difficult to respond to an order that is at once peremptory, immediate and overriding.

Examples of successful bridge-blowing operations are the demolition of the Obercaeral Bridge on the Rhine, as US troops approached on 2 March 1945, and the destruction of the Arnhem rail bridge in front of 2 Para on 17 September 1944. Such operations do not always go according to plan, however, as the failures at the Sittang Bridge in Burma in February 1942 and at the Remagen Bridge on the Rhine in March 1945 illustrate.

Timing is everything, and the success or failure of the whole operation may easily hang on a split-second decision. The key personnel must be both competent and confident – the middle of a withdrawal is no time for hesitation.

RESERVE BRIDGE DEMOLITION

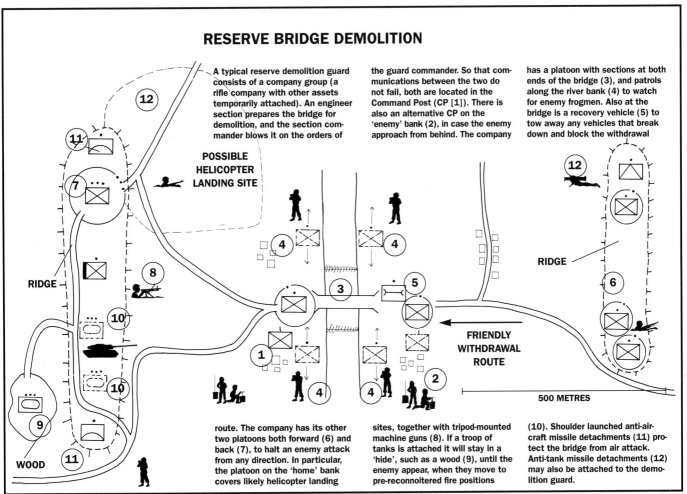

A typical reserve demolition guard consists of a company group (a rifle company with other assets temporarily attached). An engineer section prepares the bridge for demolition, and the section commander blows it on the orders of the guard commander. So that communications between the two do not fail, both are located in the Command Post (CP [1]). There is also an alternative CP on the 'enemy' bank (2), in case the enemy approach from behind. The company has a platoon with sections at both ends of the bridge (3), and patrols along the river bank (4) to watch for enemy frogmen. Also at the bridge is a recovery vehicle (5) to tow away any vehicles that break down and block the withdrawal route. The company has its other two platoons both forward (6) and back (7), to halt an enemy attack from any direction. In particular, the platoon on the 'home' bank covers likely helicopter landing sites, together with tripod-mounted machine guns (8). If a troop of tanks is attached it will stay in a 'hide', such as a wood (9), until the enemy appear, when they move to pre-reconnoitered fire positions (10). Shoulder launched anti-aircraft missile detachments (11) protect the bridge from air attack. Anti-tank missile detachments (12) may also be attached to the demolition guard.

POSSIBLE HELICOPTER LANDING SITE

RIDGE

RIDGE

FRIENDLY WITHDRAWAL ROUTE

500 METRES

WOOD

WAYS OF LAYING MINES

With the mine plough (A), the mine passes down a conveyor belt (2), where it is fuzed and then fed into a furrow made by a plough at the front of the trailer (3). Two discs at the back of the trailer then cover the mine with earth (4), and a trailing chain smoothes over the top.

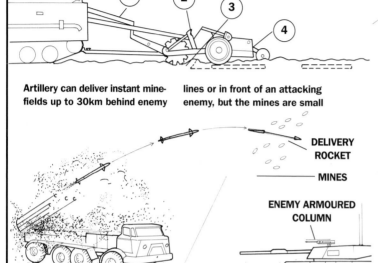

Artillery can deliver instant minefields up to 30km behind enemy lines or in front of an attacking enemy, but the mines are small

DELIVERY ROCKET

MINES

ENEMY ARMOURED COLUMN

For even faster laying of minefields, mines can be fired from projectors on helicopters and vehicles, but these are smaller than those laid by ploughs

The simplest, and slowest, way to lay mines is by hand. This usually ensures the best concealment

ment rather than men in this context – is selected and brought into play. On the fast-moving battlefield of the future this shortcoming promises to be extremely serious, as the engineers will find it hard to get sufficient advance warning of future tasks.

The over-riding question is whether or not future 'defensive' engineers will be able to obstruct and block battlefield movement so effectively that operations will cease to be fast moving at all. Will the 'offensive' engineers be able to maintain momentum? Or will they find the sheer scale of obstacles so great that the battle bogs down into immobility, as it did in World War I, in Normandy and in the Iran-Iraq War of the 1980s? It appears that the capacity of engineers to construct obstacles is increasing faster than the capacity of engineers to overcome them. If present trends are projected into the future, therefore, the engineers will become truly 'the decisive arm', insofar as they will be able to make the battlefield all but impassable. This will certainly be so if tracked or wheeled vehicles continue to be the main instruments of future mobility, for such vehicles are the engineers' primary victims and are especially vulnerable to obstacles and mines.

The helicopter, skipping blithely over the traps laid for terrestrial vehicles, is largely immune to engineering 'solutions'. However, it is worth remembering that even in the 1960s, the Viet Cong were already laying anti-helicopter 'windmill' mines

Right: Men of the Royal Engineers operating a bar mine laying vehicle reckon to install up to 600 mines an hour by this method, which has the advantage of placing the munitions in exactly the desired position. On top of the vehicle is a mine-scattering device which operates even faster, but less precisely

Below: Most engineering vehicles are optimised for more than one task. The combat engineering vehicle on the left is fitted with a mine plough and mounts a short-barrelled demolition gun, while the mobile bridge unit is also equipped with a plough

around probable US LZs. These mines are equipped with a small propellor on a vertically-mounted shaft that starts to turn only when there is a strong down-draught, such as that created by the rotors of a helicopter. The rotation of the blade triggers the mine. Another approach was to booby-trap corrugated metal sheets laid out on likely LZs. For the moment, though, the helicopter has tactical problems of its own. It's not yet in a position to seriously challenge tanks and IFVs for the title of primary battle vehicle.

Most combat engineering tasks can be accomplished with civilian tools

Back on the ground, it is clear that civilian earth-moving plant has obvious uses in military engineering operations – particularly in a war fought within a developed nation. There are specialised military machines of this type, such as the British combat engineering tractor (CET) and the US Rome Plow, a bulldozer used in Vietnam to cut away jungle cover alongside roads, but a quick look around today's motorway construction sites or major housing developments reveals that modern civil engineers use vast amounts of heavy-duty earth-moving and landscaping equipment. Today the countryside is positively littered with powerful machines, such as back-hoes, graders, diggers, motor shovels and – especially – bulldozers, with which even a few men can move and re-distribute tonnes of earth in a short space of time. Almost all of these machines would be requisitioned on a battlefield of the future, and deployed within only a few days, building successive layers of anti-tank ditches, fire positions and strongpoints ahead of an attacking enemy spearhead.

The simple anti-tank ditch has not lost its attraction, since the tank's ability to cross such obstacles

has improved not at all since 1916. If anything, the opposite is true, for the tanks of World War I were, after all, specifically designed for that task.

Provided effective fire covers the physical obstacle, the would-be assailant can be prevented from bringing forward his own engineer plant to bridge, fill or breach the gap. A dramatic illustration of this was provided on the Golan heights in 1973, where an Israeli anti-tank ditch halted Syrian armour. When the Syrians brought forward scissors bridges to cross the gap, they quickly became priority targets. Then, when one of the bridges was actually established, it had the effect of drawing all the tanks towards it, thus channelling them into a narrow area that rapidly became a killing zone.

Even quite small obstacles, covered by fire, present a huge problem

Of course, things are not always that simple. Also in the October 1973 War, first the Egyptians (on 9 October) and then the Israelis (on 15/16 October) crossed the much bigger anti-tank obstacle of the Suez Canal. In neither case, however, did the defenders cover the crossing sites effectively with fire. The Egyptian operation at the very start of the war was able to exploit strategic surprise, massive fire superiority and the poor positioning of defending strongpoints in the Bar Lev Line.

Above: The cheapest way to clear and neutralise mines is by hand. Metal detectors have been in use for almost 50 years, but the new generation of mines have so few metal parts that they are undetectable by these means

Right: It's a simple enough matter to fit MTBs with mine ploughs, and use them to clear a way through anti-personnel minefields for an infantry advance. They are even effective against the older types of anti-tank mine

Left: The Americans lost almost 60,000 men in Vietnam. The name of every one is inscribed on the Vietnam Veterans' Memorial, a wall of polished black marble in Washington DC. In front of it stands a statue of three infantrymen: one Anglo-Saxon, one Black and one Hispanic. The monument has become a place of pilgrimage for Americans, with as many visitors as longer-established sites in Washington such as the Lincoln Memorial.

TRIAGE

Triage – division into three categories – is a time-honoured principle of military medicine. In what might be called 'normal' times a field aid post will try to give maximum care and attention to all its patients; but if it comes under heavy pressure from large numbers of casualties, as the British did at San Carlos for a time during the Falklands war of 1982, a system of priorities may have to be applied.

This system is the triage, and under it the wounded will be divided into those who seem certain to die, those who can be saved with difficulty, and those who are only lightly wounded. Resources will be concentrated on the middle category, while patients in the other two will merely be made comfortable. The system is intended to ensure that the maximum number of casualties will be saved.

The same principle applies to vehicles and equipment – for instance, damaged AFVs – though here just two categories are used. A front-line unit's repair facilities may concentrate solely on those that can be put back on the road within 24 hours. The rest may either be cannibalised for spare parts, or sent back to a rear area repair shop, depending on the resources available and the state of the roads.

features – but they are also features that may spell grim death to combatants and non-combatants alike.

Recent US research has concentrated on developing safe ways to handle these weapons. Binary systems, composed of two chemicals that are harmless when stored separately in shells or rockets, but combine on impact to form nerve gas, are particularly popular. Modern nerve agents can be made non-persistent, to allow friendly forces to use the ground within half an hour of a CW attack. But for other tasks, such as airfield denial, the older, persistent type of gas would still find favour with many. In windy, rainy conditions these may remain dangerous for up to 36 hours, but in cold and calm weather they could be lethal for as long as four months.

Chemical weapons used in Europe would treble civilian casualties

As far as civilians are concerned, chemical warfare spells disaster. Civilians do not have access to the protective suits and decontamination equipment enjoyed by soldiers. It has been calculated that a war in Europe that called on chemical weapons would treble the number of civilian casualties that might be expected in a conventional conflict. It may be that civilians would rarely find themselves in areas that had been specifically targeted, but even so the chemicals would soon spill out of the battlefield into populated areas – for they are notoriously easily affected by the vagaries of the weather.

There is another problem with civilian casualties, insofar as they are not usually assessed, reported or commemorated with quite the same attention to detail that is lavished upon casualties who happen to be wearing uniform. Soldiers who are killed in action (KIA) come from a bureaucracy that is expert at taking roll calls and checking rosters of those on active duty every day. But the average

civilian town may keep only relatively vague annual lists of telephone subscribers, householders or taxpayers. Soldiers wear metallic 'dog-tags' to identify them, while civilians rarely carry anything more durable than flammable plastic credit cards or paper driving licenses.

More important still is the difference in the symbolic and political significance of a soldier who 'offers the ultimate sacrifice', and a civilian who just 'got caught in the crossfire'. In low intensity warfare, the press may raise a storm over the latter while ignoring the former; but the situation is entirely reversed as soon as the warfare increases in intensity. The fallen soldier will then be held up

Above: South African troops, fighting with Montgomery's Eighth Army during the North African campaign, prepare to clear a house. Whenever fighting comes to built-up areas, the amount of collateral damage sustained is enormous Right: Aerial and artillery bombardment can turn an inhabited area into a desert. This is Heligoland after the Allies took it in 1945

THE SCALE OF BATTLE

The size and duration of individual battles has increased considerably. The battlefield at Agincourt (A) was 500 metres wide, the engagement took just six hours, and cost 20,000 lives. Waterloo (B) took place over a four-kilometre front, lasted for 10 hours, and cost 65,000 dead. By 1916, and the Battle of the Somme (C), the fighting front was almost 50km long, the battle lasted for four and a half months, and the death toll was 1,200,000 men. The Battle of Normandy (D), which started with the D-Day landings on 6 June 1944, ranged over 120km, took 10 weeks, and cost 450,000 casualties

ANTI-PERSONNEL MUNITIONS

The changeover from large single anti-personnel bombs to cluster munitions means that there is far less energy wasted in sending fragments high up in to the air, where they do no good. A cluster bomb covers a larger area much more economically

NOTES
The outer semi-circle denotes the lethal area of a 250lb fragmentation bomb.
Each of the smaller semi-circles represents the lethal area of a modern cluster sub-munition or hand grenade.
The dotted line shows the range of a modern grenade launcher. The 150m semi-circle shows the lethal area of a modern defensive grenade, while the inner semi-circle shows the lethal area of a WWII Mills Bomb

Each bomblet has the same effect as an infantry grenade – a destructive radius of perhaps 75 metres. Even a good ball player would have trouble throwing a grenade that far, so the light-weight launcher was developed to project a grenade up to 250 metres

150 m

600 m

as a shining example for succeeding generations, while the civilian victim may often appear more as an unwelcome reproach against a government that has failed to protect him.

Civilian wounded are also likely to be cared for less effectively than soldiers wounded in action (WIA). The reason is that civilian hospitals generally have fewer facilities for sudden influxes of wounded than do the medical echelons in advanced armies – and if the armies are already fully occupied with their own WIA they will have no surplus capacity left over for civilians.

Modern warfare produces more burns than gunshot wounds

Military medicine has made huge advances in the last three decades. Vietnam showed how rapid helicopter casualty evacuation ('medevac' or 'casevac') can save the lives of unprecedented numbers of WIA: estimates of the survival rate among the wounded airlifted from Vietnam battlefields range from 82 to 98 per cent, though we can never know how many of them would have been saved by treatment in situ followed by surface evacuation.

Advances in civilian medicine have also spun-off benefits for those WIA. Ultrasonic scanners, for example, can help locate plastic shrapnel fragments that fail to show up on X-ray. In the Falklands war of 1982 the survival rate of WIA was increased still

Above: The Americans' Hearts and Minds programme in Vietnam attempted – with limited success – to establish bonds of trust and acceptance between themselves and the indigenous population

Right: The airborne gunships, Spooky, Shadow and Spectre – based on the C-47 Dakota, the C-119 Flying Boxcar and the C-130 Hercules, respectively – proved to be terrifyingly effective as their miniguns laid down a sheet of fire that could cover every square inch of a football pitch in a matter of moments. This time-exposure photograph reveals every minigun burst as a solid stream of fire

BOMBERS AND BOMB LOADS

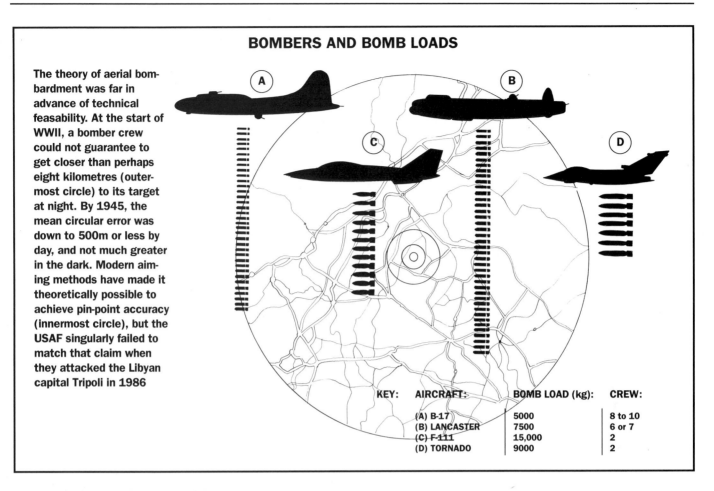

The theory of aerial bombardment was far in advance of technical feasability. At the start of WWII, a bomber crew could not guarantee to get closer than perhaps eight kilometres (outermost circle) to its target at night. By 1945, the mean circular error was down to 500m or less by day, and not much greater in the dark. Modern aiming methods have made it theoretically possible to achieve pin-point accuracy (innermost circle), but the USAF singularly failed to match that claim when they attacked the Libyan capital Tripoli in 1986

KEY:	AIRCRAFT:	BOMB LOAD (kg):	CREW:
(A)	B-17	5000	8 to 10
(B)	LANCASTER	7500	6 or 7
(C)	F-111	15,000	2
(D)	TORNADO	9000	2

further by advances in the treatment of wounds gained in the Royal Victoria Hospital, Belfast, during the Northern Ireland 'troubles'. Still more important, a very high level of first aid training among all the infantry soldiers meant that instead of a single medic per platoon there were effectively 30, yet how many soldiers are going to take time out of the battle to come to the aid of a wounded civilian?

The sensitivity to any friendly casualties is noticeably rising

Some concern about civilian casualties in modern warfare may be misplaced. It is actually possible that modern improvements in weaponry will not, after all, bring an overall increase in the numbers of either killed or wounded per day of combat. We should recognise that the fearsomeness of many of these weapons has more to do with media hype than it does with reality. This comes about not just through the arms industry's own self-serving advertising – which is prodigious – but also through the appetite of the media for new sensational stories.

Technological warfare, almost by definition, originates in highly developed societies where life is relatively soft. Such societies have an escalating horror of all forms of hardship, destruction and death, and their sensitivity to any hostile weaponry or friendly casualties is noticeably rising, especially when the casualties are 'innocent civilians' and, perhaps surprisingly, even when they are professional soldiers whose stock in trade is death and destruction.

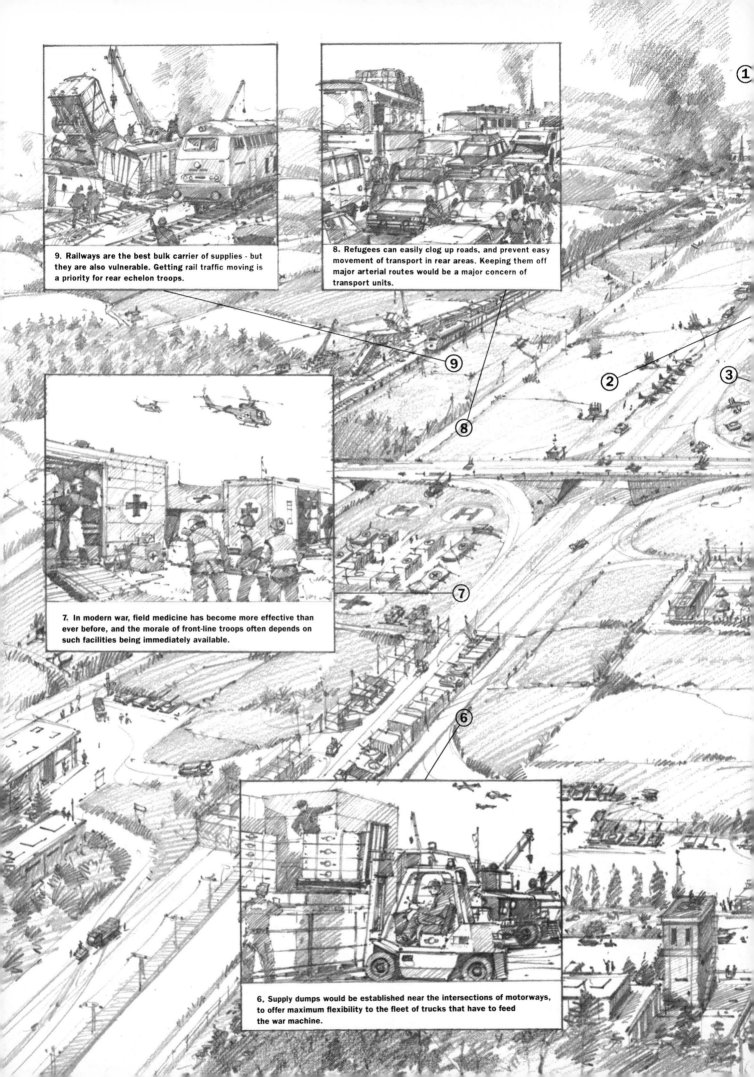

9. Railways are the best bulk carrier of supplies - but they are also vulnerable. Getting rail traffic moving is a priority for rear echelon troops.

8. Refugees can easily clog up roads, and prevent easy movement of transport in rear areas. Keeping them off major arterial routes would be a major concern of transport units.

7. In modern war, field medicine has become more effective than ever before, and the morale of front-line troops often depends on such facilities being immediately available.

6. Supply dumps would be established near the intersections of motorways, to offer maximum flexibility to the fleet of trucks that have to feed the war machine.

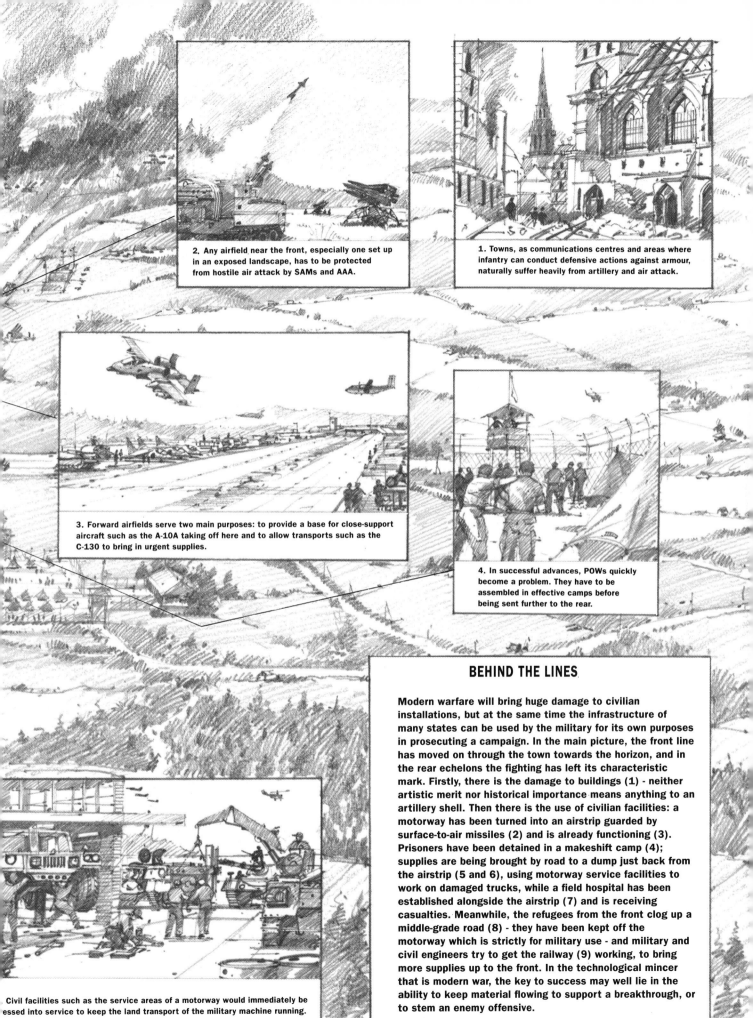

2. Any airfield near the front, especially one set up in an exposed landscape, has to be protected from hostile air attack by SAMs and AAA.

1. Towns, as communications centres and areas where infantry can conduct defensive actions against armour, naturally suffer heavily from artillery and air attack.

3. Forward airfields serve two main purposes: to provide a base for close-support aircraft such as the A-10A taking off here and to allow transports such as the C-130 to bring in urgent supplies.

4. In successful advances, POWs quickly become a problem. They have to be assembled in effective camps before being sent further to the rear.

BEHIND THE LINES

Modern warfare will bring huge damage to civilian installations, but at the same time the infrastructure of many states can be used by the military for its own purposes in prosecuting a campaign. In the main picture, the front line has moved on through the town towards the horizon, and in the rear echelons the fighting has left its characteristic mark. Firstly, there is the damage to buildings (1) - neither artistic merit nor historical importance means anything to an artillery shell. Then there is the use of civilian facilities: a motorway has been turned into an airstrip guarded by surface-to-air missiles (2) and is already functioning (3). Prisoners have been detained in a makeshift camp (4); supplies are being brought by road to a dump just back from the airstrip (5 and 6), using motorway service facilities to work on damaged trucks, while a field hospital has been established alongside the airstrip (7) and is receiving casualties. Meanwhile, the refugees from the front clog up a middle-grade road (8) - they have been kept off the motorway which is strictly for military use - and military and civil engineers try to get the railway (9) working, to bring more supplies up to the front. In the technological mincer that is modern war, the key to success may well lie in the ability to keep material flowing to support a breakthrough, or to stem an enemy offensive.

Civil facilities such as the service areas of a motorway would immediately be essed into service to keep the land transport of the military machine running.

This relatively modern perception can seriously distort policy-making and strategy. For example: the USA was persuaded to pull out of Vietnam mainly because of the 20,000 dead she had suffered in the four years leading up to the Tet Offensive of 1968, even though she was claiming to have inflicted around twenty times that total on the enemy – not all of whom, it was suspected even at the time, were necessarily combatants. In 1973 Israel was deeply unhappy with the result of the Yom Kippur war when she lost 3000 dead as the price of a double victory, over both Egypt and Syria. She had been hoping, perhaps, for a result closer to that of June 1967: around 1000 dead in return for a spectacular doubling of her territory.

Advancing armies always spread a wave of terror ahead of them

The most tragic feature of the modern battlefield is perhaps the flood of refugees, evacuees, orphans and displaced persons that it generates. Advancing armies always spread a wave of terror ahead of them, and this is likely to become more intense in future. The proliferation of civilian news media might be expected to contribute to the spread of terror in a war zone, but this is unlikely to be the case; these (VHF) means of

Right: One notable feature of modern conflict is the number of friendly nationals caught up in hostilities on foreign soil. The US Air Force airlifted many US citizens out of Grenada after the island was invaded

communication will be rendered inoperable by electronic warfare even more quickly than will military communications.

Nevertheless, the lifestyles and expectations of civilian populations in developed countries, and their massive access to motor vehicles, will tend to create both a greater desire to escape and a more widespread attempt to do so. Something of this sort was seen in the prompt Catholic exodus from Belfast in August 1969, in response to an outbreak of violence that – by comparison with the harsh standards of wholesale conventional warfare – can only be described as minor.

Pitiful streams of refugees were a heart-rending feature of many European campaigns during World War II. They have often reappeared in subsequent conflicts, such as the Arab-Israeli war of 1967 or the American war in Vietnam. The scale and intensity of the refugee problem will surely be greater in any future conflict that takes place in industrialised countries – and from the armies' point of view this will be significant in two very different ways.

In the first scenario the sad columns of refugees may be treated as unfortunate victims of an unfortunate circumstance: helpless people to be succoured and aided in every way possible, even if – irritatingly to distant staff officers – they block roads and interrupt military operations. This was a problem for

the Western allies during the 1940 campaign in France, when the Germans, it was suggested, tried to create tactical obstacles by deliberately herding refugees into traffic nodes, such as cross-roads, using fighter ground attack (FGA) aircraft to nudge them along with regular strafings.

In any future war this traffic problem would be greatly intensified, just because the sheer volume of traffic of all kinds, military or civilian, will be so much greater. However, the first few passes by modern FGA planes – which might charitably be expected to be seeking purely military targets – may well clear major roads of absolutely all traffic, regardless of its origins or its intentions.

A refugee needs just as much food and shelter as a combat soldier

When, during World War II, the Allies invaded Italy, France and then Germany herself, the Western armies accepted considerable tactical disruption because of their soldiers' generally well-meaning relations with civilians. A refugee needs just as much food and shelter as a combat soldier or a prisoner of war (POW), and the Western Allies' resources were seriously stretched by their policy of taking whatever care they could of the disrupted civilian population. Nevertheless, they felt it was

LETHALITY v LOSSES			
BATTLE & DATE	**CASUALTIES (both sides combined)**	**DAYS**	**CASUALTIES (per day)**
Borodino 1812	74,000	1	74,000
Leipzig 1813	127,000	4	31,750
Waterloo 1815	63,000	1	63,000
Antietam 1862	22,000	1	22,000
Gettysburg 1863	45,000	3	15,000
Gravelotte 1870	33,000	1	33,000
Somme 1916 First day:	61,000	1	61,000
Whole battle	1,200,000	140	8571
Verdun 1916	750,000	300	2500
2nd Alamein 1942	35,000	12	2916
October War 1973 Syrian front:	7000	19	370
Canal front:	11,000	19	579
Total in war:	18,000	19	949
Lebanon Invasion 1982	11,000	70	157

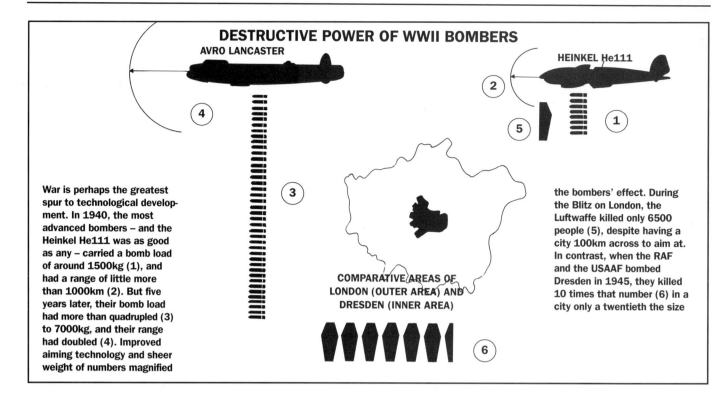

DESTRUCTIVE POWER OF WWII BOMBERS

AVRO LANCASTER

HEINKEL He111

War is perhaps the greatest spur to technological development. In 1940, the most advanced bombers – and the Heinkel He111 was as good as any – carried a bomb load of around 1500kg (1), and had a range of little more than 1000km (2). But five years later, their bomb load had more than quadrupled (3) to 7000kg, and their range had doubled (4). Improved aiming technology and sheer weight of numbers magnified

COMPARATIVE AREAS OF
LONDON (OUTER AREA) AND
DRESDEN (INNER AREA)

the bombers' effect. During the Blitz on London, the Luftwaffe killed only 6500 people (5), despite having a city 100km across to aim at. In contrast, when the RAF and the USAAF bombed Dresden in 1945, they killed 10 times that number (6) in a city only a twentieth the size

---

only proper to devote considerable manpower, and a major administrative effort, to civilian government and rehabilitation. This consisted of 'G5' staffwork functions, which imposed unexpected non-tactical pressures on the military, not to mention the far-reaching political implications that were involved for the future state of Europe.

The whole problem of refugees is a major burden to any fighting army

There were occasions when the Allied commanders deliberately avoided targets of enormous psychological significance simply because of the drain that the dislocation and disruption to the civilian population would have imposed on their fighting resources. It has even been suggested that Allied Supreme Commander Dwight D. Eisenhower resisted the flamboyant, francophile General George Smith Patton's insistent demands that he be allowed to march on Paris (as he could easily have done) for just that reason. Eisenhower was aware that feeding the population of Paris would have starved his own troops, and so he planned to bypass the city. Other commentators have a more romantic explanation: that the honour should fall to the men of the Free French Army. In the event, the people of Paris rose and liberated themselves – leaving the French capital to be entered, in due course, by General Jacques Leclerc's Second French Division, and French civil problems to be shouldered by Frenchmen.

In Vietnam, the Americans made great efforts to avoid fighting in built-up areas if they could possibly help it; but even in rural areas they were seriously embarrassed by the large masses of refugees that the war created. Vast tracts of the country became depopulated, with tactical maps being dotted with the word 'abandoned' beside many a hamlet.

There can be no doubt that the whole problem of refugees – even if it is to some extent actually a self-created problem – is a major and most unwelcome burden to any fighting army. Soldiers do not feel happy when they are in close proximity to civilians, especially unhappy civilians.

The problem is far worse for the civilians, however, in the second scenario for civil-military relations within a war zone. This is the still bleaker prospect of an invading army that sees itself as a positive scourge upon an alien and hostile population. In this case there is an assumption of unadorned power. The invading army invades and rules, while the local population is expected to cringe, turn its face to the wall, and simply accept its fate. The invading army may inflict almost limitless atrocities and indignities upon its victims, as did first the German army in Russia and then in turn the Russian army in Germany, during World War II.

The Khmer Rouge have exploited refugees with ruthless cynicism

In these circumstances any column of refugees may look to a prejudiced army much more like a 'legitimate target' than an 'innocent victim'. There is probably no army in the world that can honestly say that, under the stress, frustration and frequent ambiguity of 20th-Century combat, it has never at some time or another turned its guns on entirely innocent civilians.

The moral and practical difficulties and dangers faced by both military and civilians in conflicts where the enemy depends absolutely on the civil population for its sustenance have been illustrated with chilling clarity by such incidents as the massacre of Vietnamese men, women and children at My Lai in March 1968 and the slaughter of Palestinians by Lebanese Christian militia at Chabra

The current spate of 'troubles' in Ulster is now in to its third decade. An entire generation has grown up in the Province without ever knowing the true meaning of peace. From one side of the Province to the other – from Derry's Bogside (Top) to Belfast's Divis Flats (Right) – the helicopter and the armoured car are an accepted part of everyday life

ground-to-air and air-to-air weapons than the IFV is to AT weapons. Helicopters may well be admirably suited to wearing down a tank attack as snipers or as reconnaissance fire controllers, but they surely cannot hope to survive very long as infantry transport much beyond the enemy's front line, and certainly not in the absence of air superiority.

As for artillery, the future battlefield promises to be completely dominated by long-range indirect fire. The 'deep battle' is a vital part of modern artillery practice, and can now be conducted with devastating accuracy. Gun and rocket fire will scour through what used to be the enemy's secure rear area, and will extend the battlefield 70km or more beyond the FLOT. The main problems facing the guns – and so many other new weapons – will be surveillance and logistics. Just as our guns will be able to see deep into the enemy's rear, so the enemy will be able to see them and pick them off. And the quicker they can identify targets, the quicker they're likely to expend their precious loads of ammunition.

Provided they can avoid the attention of artillery, engineers will be able to make even greater changes to the future battlefield than they could ever have done in the past. Massed ranks of earth movers will create deep layers of anti-tank

ditches and bunkers; minelayers will go forward to create lethal obstacles, and tree blowdowns will soon make any forest impassable. Against this kind of prepared battlefield it is hard to see how any mechanised army can possibly hope to move.

The most advanced weaponry may well prove to be unworkable

There are at least three key factors that may unblock this apparent log jam. Perhaps the most likely is that one side will run out of resources much sooner than the other. Unlike the situation that occurred in 1915, the 'shell shortage' in a future war may not apply to both sides simultaneously. The side with sufficient reserves of ammunition and POL will then continue to press its attack. The army left in this fortunate position may not be the most advanced technologically, however: the rate of consumption of supplies promises to be much higher with sophisticated weapons than with more basic ones.

Second, it may well turn out that the most advanced weaponry proves to be unworkable. Peacetime armies swelled out to their wartime establishment by conscripts and volunteers may lack sufficient numbers of adequately skilled soldiers to keep

Left: Gone are the days when the infantrymen had to guess at the range of their target. Now, laser rangefinders such as this reel off the distance to the nearest metre, as far as the amplified eye can see

Left: Static installations, such as airfields, have always qualified for a higher standard of protection. Rapier, shown here, is acknowledged to be one of the best of the medium-range surface-to-air missile systems. There is also a vehicle-mounted system in service with the British Army and the RAF, which extends the weapon's umbrella right up to the forward edge of the battle area

THE SHRINKING WEAPON

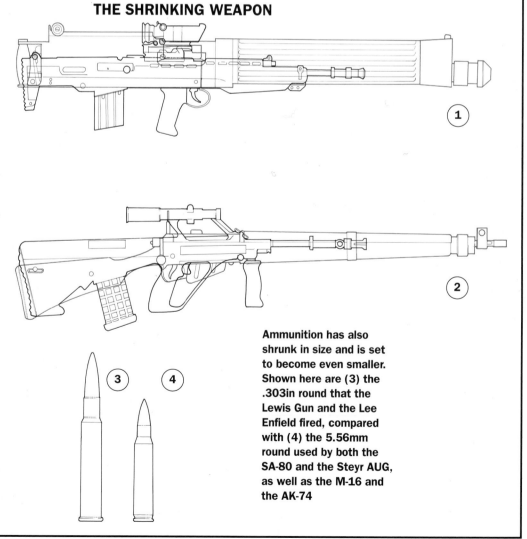

Right: Infantry weapons are getting progressively smaller, and therefore lighter, as better and better propellant charges are developed; for the killing power of a bullet is determined by two factors – its mass, and the speed at which it impacts with the target. The faster the bullet travels, the lighter it can be, but still inflict the same degree of damage

Over the course of the 20th Century, both the machine gun and the rifle have have shrunk in size by more than 50 per cent, and the rounds they fire have become even smaller. Shown here (1) is the SA-80, superimposed upon a Lewis Gun, which was the British Army's staple automatic weapon, circa 1918; also shown (2) is a Steyr AUG superimposed upon a Mark 4 Lee Enfield rifle, which saw service until the late 1950s

Ammunition has also shrunk in size and is set to become even smaller. Shown here are (3) the .303in round that the Lewis Gun and the Lee Enfield fired, compared with (4) the 5.56mm round used by both the SA-80 and the Steyr AUG, as well as the M-16 and the AK-74

Aircraft, too, are changing their shape. If the F-117A Stealth Fighter seems outlandish, it's a fair bet that tomorrow's aircraft will be even more extreme. Above: MacDonnell Douglas's contender for the next generation of multi-role fighter aircraft, the YF-23, is not designed to the same criteria as the F-117 at all, yet it has some of the same lines

the equipment working properly, and there may not be the time in war to train new experts to keep pace with combat losses. The battlefield may break apart simply because of a shortage of skills. And the technology itself may prove unsatisfactory. In 1967 and 1968 the much-heralded dawn of electronic battlefield surveillance in Vietnam turned out to be something of a damp squib. In the 1973 October War, the equally trumpeted ATGW 'revolution' also produced disappointing final statistics. Primitive bazookas proved to be better tank killers than sophisticated wire-guided missiles. Such experiences should lead us to treat the claims of the weapons manufacturers with – at the very least – considerable caution.

Third, a very effective answer to trenchlock may be found in the traditional methods of deception and surprise, or *maskirovka*. This can allow highly mobile spearheads to penetrate deep into an unsuspecting opponent's territory before he has a chance to set up his firepower and obstacles. The best technological weaponry in the world is useless if its operators are unaware that they are at war with anyone. The best air force will be grounded if its runways are cratered and mined before the aircraft have taken off. Nor will even overwhelming numerical superiority help a defender who has already been overrun by the time his troops manage to struggle out of their barracks.

If there should be a high-technology war in the 1990s, its early days will see many mistakes. Key items may be missing from the inventories, and weapons that exist only on paper may be urgently

needed on the battlefield. The soldiers who have to use the most advanced weapons may not understand them fully, which will hinder still further their ability to break through the enemy's position. However, if the war continues long enough the armies will learn new tricks, and will find how to get the best out of what is available. There will also be crash development programmes and a mobilisation of scientific and industrial talent. We may then see not just the present new generation of weaponry deployed in the field, but its successor as well.

WWI was horrific, but casualties were light by modern standards

Just what will that next generation of technology look like? Doubtless there will be a continuing enhancement of 'smart' indirect-fire artillery, and a final realisation of the truly deep battle at long range. Airfields may become a thing of the past, and an army's whole rear area, previously regarded as secure, may be right in the firing line. On the other hand, incoming missiles and warheads may be vulnerable to rapidly reacting point defences, perhaps using DEW or electromagnetic rail guns. Then again, the RPV and the remotely-controlled tank will surely be able to fire without exposing the location of their human operators. And, perhaps even more important, a proliferation of stealth technologies will go far towards restoring the classic 'empty battlefield' of the early 20th century.

BIBLIOGRAPHY

Many of the most important details for this subject appear in the military periodical press, rather than in books. Only a few of the relevant articles can be mentioned here, but in general the reader is referred especially to back numbers of *International Defense Review* for the hardware, and *Military Review* for the doctrines and tactics.

J Albright, J A Cash & A W Sandstrum, *Seven Firefights in Vietnam* (Vietnam Studies Series. Department of the Army, Washington DC 1970)

J R Alford, *Mobile Defense, the Pervasive Myth* — (King's College thesis, London 1977)

Anon, *Lessons of Lebanon* in *Defence Attache* No 4, 1982, p23 ff

Anon, *Operations: FM 100-5, 20 August 1982* (Headquarters, Department of the Army, Washington DC)

Anon, *German Defense Tactics Against Russian Break-Throughs* (US Army Department 20-233, Washington DC, October 1951)

M de Arcangelis, *Electronic Warfare* (Blandford, Poole, Dorset 1985)

J B A Bailey, *Field Artillery and Firepower* (Military Press, Oxford 1989)

F Barnaby, *The Automated Battlefield* (Sidgwick & Jackson, London 1986)

F Barnaby & M ter Borg, *Emerging Technologies and Military Doctrine* (Macmillan, London 1986)

C Bellamy, *The Future of Land Warfare* (Croom Helm, London 1987)

C Bellamy, *Red God of War* (Brassey, London 1986)

R G S Bidwell, *Gunners at War* (Arms & Armour, London 1970)

R G S Bidwell, *World War 3* (Hamlyn, London 1978) (fiction)

R G S Bidwell & D Graham, *Firepower* (Allen & Unwin, London, 1982)

J Bradley, *The Illustrated History of World War 3* (Omega, Leicester 1982)

C Campbell, *War Facts Now* (Fontana, London 1982)

T Clancy, *Red Storm Rising* (Collins, London 1987) (fiction)

H Coyle, *Team Yankee* (Presidio Press, San Novato, Calif. 1987) (fiction)

H Coyle, *Sword Point* (Penguin, London 1989) (fiction)

M Creveld, *Fighting Power* (Arms & Armour, London 1983)

P Dickson, *The Electronic Battlefield* (London 1976)

E Dinter, *Hero or Coward?* (Cass. London 1985)

E Dinter and P Griffith, *Not Over by Christmas* (Bird, Chichester 1983)

T N Dupuy, The Evolution of Weapons and Warfare (First published 1980; Jane's edn, London 1982)

J Ellis, *The Sharp End of War* (David & Charles, Newton Abbot, Devon 1980)

J A English, *On Infantry* (First published Praeger, New York 1981; new edn 1984)

ESECS, *Strengthening Conventional Deterrence in Europe*, the report of the European Security Study (Macmillan, London 1983)

C D'Este, *Decision in Normandy* (Pan edn, London 1984)

J J Ewell & I A Hunt, *Sharpening the Combat Edge* (Vietnam Studies series, Department of the Army, Washington DC 1974)

H Faringdon, *Confrontation* (RKP, London 1986)

R S Friedman, *Advanced Technology Warfare* (Salamander, London 1985)

R A Gabriel, *Military Incompetence: why the American military doesn't win* (Hill & Wang, New York 1985)

R A Gabriel, *Operation Peace for Galilee* (Hill & Wang, New York 1984)

L H Gann, ed., *The Defense of Western Europe* (Croom Helm, 1987)

P Griffith, *Forward Into Battle* (New Edn, Crowood, Ramsbury Wilts. 1990)

P Griffith, *Countering Surprise by Mobility — a concept for armoured warfare on the Central Front* in *The Sandhurst Journal of Military Studies* vol 1, no 1, 1990

B Gunston and M Spick, *Modern Fighting Helicopters* (Salamander, London 1986)

J Hackett, *The Third World War* (Sidgwick & Jackson, London 1978) (fiction)

H Halberstadt, NTC — *A Primer of Land Combat* (Presidio Press, San Novato, Calif. 1989)

N Hannig, *The Defense of Western Europe with Conventional Weapons* in *International Defense Review* vol 15, no 3, April 1982, pp 1439-1442

J P Harris & F H Toase, eds, *Armoured Warfare* (Batsford, London 1990)

J H Hay, *Tactical and Material Innovations* (Vietnam Studies series, Department of the Army, Washington DC 1974)

C Herzog, *The Arab-Israeli Wars* (Arms & Armour, London 1982)

C Herzog, *The War of Atonement* (Weidenfeld & Nicholson, London 1975)

R Holmes, *Firing Line* (Cape, London 1985. Published in USA as *Acts of War*)

Mary Kaldor, *The Baroque Arsenal* (Deutsch, London 1982)

L Lavoic, *Is the Tank Dead?* in *Defense & Diplomacy* Vol 7, No 5, May 1989, p 16

R G Lee, *Introduction to Battlefield Weapons Systems and Technology* (2nd edn, Brassey's 1985)

R Lopez, *The Airland Battle 2000 Controversy — Who is being short-sighted?* in *International Defense Review*, 1983 no 11, pp 1551-6

T T Lupfer, *The Dynamics of Doctrine: The Changes in German Tactical Doctrine During the First World War* (US Army Command and General Staff College, Fort Leavenworth, Kansas 1981)

E Luttwak & D Horrowitz, *The Israeli Army* (Lane, London 1975)

J J G Mackenzie & B H Reid (eds) *The British Army and the Operational Level of War* (Tri-Service, London 1989)

K Macksey, *Tank Warfare, a History of Tanks in Battle* (Hart-Davis, London 1971)

K Macksey, *First Clash — Combat Close-up in World War Three* (Arms and Armour, London, 1985) (fiction)

E von Manstein, *Lost Victories* (first published 1955, translated Methuen, London 1958)

J Marriott, *Weapons Technology* (RUSI and Brassey's, London 1975)

S L A Marshall, *Men Against Fire* (New York 1947)

S L A Marshall, *Infantry Operations & Weapons Usage in Korea* (E C Ezell ed, Greenhill, London 1988)

R Mason, *Chickenhawk* (first published 1983, Penguin edn, London 1984)

J J Mearsheimer, *Maneuver, Mobile Defense and the NATO Central Front* in *International Security* vol 6, no 3, winter 1981-2, pp 104-22

J J Mearsheimer, *Why the Soviets Can't Win Quickly in Central Europe* in *International Security* vol 7, no 1, Summer 1982, pp 3-39

F W von Mellenthin, *Panzer Battles* (trans

Betzler, Cassell, London 1955 and Okiahoma University 1956)

C Messenger, *Armies of World War 3* (Bison, London 1984)

D Middleton, ed, *Air War Vietnam* (USAF, reprinted London 1978)

D Miller and C F Foss, *Modern Land Combat* (Salamander, London 1987)

D M O Miller and others, *The Balance of Military Power* (Salamander, London 1981)

R Ogorkicwicz, *Countermeasures for Tanks: Beating smart munitions* in *International Defense Review* 1989, No 1

D E Ott, *Field Artillery, 1954-73* (Vietnam Studies series, Department of the Army, Washington DC 1975)

P Paret, ed., *Makers of Modern Strategy* (Princeton University, 1986)

R Peters, *Red Army* (W H Allen, London 1989) (fiction)

R L Pfaltzgraff jr. U Ra'anan, R H Shultz & I Lukes, eds, *Emerging Doctrines and Technologies* (Lexington, Mass. 1988)

A J Pierre, ed, *The Conventional Defense of Europe* (Council on Foreign Relations, New York 1986)

R R Ploger, *U S Army Engineers, 1965-70* (Vietnam Studies series, Department of the Army, Washington DC 1974)

G G Prosch, *Israeli Defense of the Golan*, an interview with Brigadier General Avigdor Kahalani in *Military Review* vol 59, no 10, Oct 1979, pp ;2-13.

U Ra'anan, *The New Technologies and the Middle East: Lessons of the Yom Kippur War and Anticipated Developments* in G Kemp et al, eds, *The Other Arms Race* (Lexington, Mass 1975), pp 79-90

W R Richardson, *FM100-5: the Air-Land Battle in 1986* in *Military Review*, vol 66, no 3, March 1986, pp 4-11

G F Rogers, *The Battle for Suez City* in *Military Review* vol 59, no 11, November 1979, pp 27-33

P Sabin, *The Third World War Scare in Britain* (Macmillan, London, 1986)

B F Schlemmer, *The Raid* (MacDonald & Jane's, London 1976)

D A Starry, *Extending the Battlefield* in *Military Review*, vol 61, no 3, March 1981, pp 32-50

D A Starry, *Mounted Combat in Vietnam* (Vietnam Studies series, Department of the Army, Washington DC 1978)

J J Tolson, *Airmobility, 1961-71* (Vietnam Studies series, Department of the Army, Washington DC 1973)

P Towle, ed., *Estimating Foreign Military Power* (Croom Helm, London 1982)

T Wintringham & J N Blashford-Snell, *Weapons and Tactics* (Pelican edn, London 1973)

Zaloga, *Red Thrust* (Brassey's, London 1989)